THE ALCHEMIST

Paulo Coelho

SPARK PUBLISHING

Spark Publishing
A Division of Barnes & Noble
120 Fifth Avenue
New York, NY 10011
www.sparknotes.com

ISBN-13: 978-1-4114-7101-6

Printed in Canada

10 9

CONTENTS

Context

Before *The Alchemist* launched him to worldwide fame, Brazilian author Paulo Coelho experienced a bumpy writing career. As a teen, Coelho, who admits he was hostile and isolated at the time, told his parents he wanted to be a writer. The untraditional career path, coupled with his behavior, led his parents to commit Coelho to a mental hospital three separate times. After this period, he relented to his parents' wishes and enrolled in law school, but dropped out after one year and became a globetrotting hippie through the 60s and 70s. During this time, Coelho published the unsuccessful *Hell Archives* (1982) and contributed to the Practical *Manual of Vampirism* (1985), but he mostly immersed himself in the drug culture and penned song lyrics for Brazilian pop stars such as Elis Regina, Rita Lee, and Raul Seixas. Despite his lack of success writing books, Coelho made good money as a lyricist. He could have easily made this his career, but a trip to Spain pointed him down a different path.

This turning point in Coelho's writing career came in 1982, when he walked Spain's road of Santiago de Compostela, or the Way of Saint James, an important medieval Christian pilgrimage route. During the walk, Coelho had a spiritual awakening that he chronicled in his second novel, *The Pilgrimage* (1987). The book had little impact, but Coelho became determined to make a career as a writer. Coelho found the concept for his next book, *The Alchemist* (1988) in a 1935 short story by Argentinean writer Jorge Luis Borges called "Tale of Two Dreamers." Like *The Alchemist*, Borges's short story revolves around two dreamers in search of treasure. Coelho sold his book to a tiny Brazilian publishing house, which printed a minuscule first edition of 900 copies and decided not to reprint afterward.

The Alchemist achieved commercial success only after Coelho found a bigger publisher, Rocco, to publish his next book, *Brida* (1990). *Brida* received good press coverage in Brazil, and Coelho's newfound popularity launched *The Alchemist* to the top of the Brazilian bestseller list. In 1993, U.S. publisher HarperCollins decided to print *The Alchemist*, starting with a print run of 50,000 copies. Though that number was significant at the time, it did not compare with the astounding success the book would eventually have. Since its U.S. publication, *The Alchemist* has won the

Guinness World Record for the most translated book by a living author. It has been translated into 67 languages, has sold over 65 million copies throughout the world, and has won several international awards, including France's Grand Prix Litteraire Elle in 1995, Germany's 2002 Corine International Award for fiction, and the United Kingdom's 2004 Nielsen Gold Book Award.

The unprecedented success of *The Alchemist* launched Coelho to international literary fame and, in some circles, notoriety. He has won celebrity fans from Bill Clinton to Will Smith to Madonna, and has written more than twenty commercially successful books since *The Alchemist,* many of which have been inspired by his own life experiences. Despite Coelho's success, he has his fair share of detractors. Several writers and critics, including the Brazilian critic Mario Maestri, accuse him of producing mass-market self-help fables disguised as literature. Coelho has also distinguished himself by his willingness to share his books over the Internet for free. His American publisher caught him pirating his own books over several popular torrent sites and forced him to stop the practice. In return, the publisher allowed each of his new books to be available on its website for free for one month after being released in stores.

Clear connections exist between the story of *The Alchemist* and Coelho's own life story. Just like Santiago, a comfortable shepherd who decided to abandon everything to pursue a dream, Coelho was living comfortably as a songwriter when he decided to give up everything to pursue his dream of writing. Just as Santiago suffered many setbacks and temptations during his journey to Egypt's pyramids, Coelho suffered a number of setbacks, including the disappointing reception of *The Pilgrimage* and the initial failure of *The Alchemist,* and experienced material temptations arising from his financial success as a songwriter. Yet, just like Santiago, Coelho remained focused on his dream, eventually achieving literary success beyond his expectations. Interestingly, Coelho didn't gain fame and financial success as an author until well after writing *The Alchemist.* Although Coelho's subsequent success more than validates the lesson he communicates through the story of Santiago's journey, success such as Santiago finds in *The Alchemist* was something Coelho had yet to attain at the time he wrote the book.

PLOT OVERVIEW

A recurring dream troubles Santiago, a young and adventurous Andalusian shepherd. He has the dream every time he sleeps under a sycamore tree that grows out of the ruins of a church. During the dream, a child tells him to seek treasure at the foot of the Egyptian pyramids. Santiago consults a gypsy woman to interpret the dream, and to his surprise she tells him to go to Egypt. A strange, magical old man named Melchizedek, who claims to be the King of Salem, echoes the gypsy's advice and tells Santiago that it is his Personal Legend to journey to the pyramids. Melchizedek convinces Santiago to sell his flock and set off to Tangier. When Santiago arrives in Tangier, a thief robs him, forcing him to find work with a local crystal merchant. The conservative and kindly merchant teaches Santiago several lessons, and Santiago encourages the merchant to take risks with his business. The risks pay off and Santiago becomes a rich man in just a year.

Santiago decides to cash in his earnings and continue pursuing his Personal Legend: to find treasure at the pyramids. He joins a caravan crossing the Sahara Desert toward Egypt and meets an Englishman who is studying to become an alchemist. He learns a lot from the Englishman during the journey. For one thing, he learns that the secret of alchemy is written on a stone called the Emerald Tablet. The ultimate creation of alchemy is the Master Work, which consists of a solid called the Philosopher's Stone that can turn lead to gold, and a liquid called the Elixir of Life that can cure all ills. Santiago learns the Englishman is traveling with the caravan to the Saharan oasis of Al-Fayoum, where a powerful, 200-year-old alchemist resides. The Englishman plans to ask the alchemist the secret of his trade. Santiago joins the caravan.

As it turns out, the caravan must make an extended stop in Al-Fayoum in order to avoid increasingly violent tribal wars taking place in the desert. There, Santiago falls in love with Fatima, who lives at the oasis. During a walk in the desert, Santiago witnesses an omen that portends an attack on the historically neutral oasis. He warns the tribal chieftains of the attack, and as a result, Al-Fayoum successfully defends itself against the assault. The alchemist gets word of Santiago's vision and invites Santiago on a trip into the desert, during which he teaches Santiago about the importance of listening to his heart and pursuing his Personal Legend. He convinces Santiago to leave Fatima and the caravan for a time to finish his journey to the pyramids, and he offers to accompany Santiago on the next leg of his trip.

While the alchemist and Santiago travel through the desert, the alchemist shares much of his wisdom about the Soul of the World. They are mere days away from the pyramids when a tribe of Arab soldiers captures them. In exchange for his life and the life of Santiago, the alchemist hands over to the tribe all of Santiago's money and tells the soldiers that Santiago is a powerful alchemist who will turn into wind within three days. Santiago feels alarmed because he has no idea how to turn into the wind, and over the next three days he contemplates the desert. On the third day, he communicates with the wind and the sun and coaxes them to help him create a tremendous sandstorm. He prays to the Hand That Wrote All, and at the height of the storm he disappears. He reappears on the other side of the camp, and the tribesmen, awed by the power of the storm and by Santiago's ability, let him and the alchemist go free.

The alchemist continues to travel with Santiago as far as a Coptic monastery several hours from the pyramids. There he demonstrates to Santiago his ability to turn lead into gold using the Philosopher's Stone. He gives Santiago gold and sends him off. Santiago begins digging for the treasure at the foot of the pyramids, but two men accost him and beat him. When Santiago speaks to them about his dream vision, they decide he must have no money and let him live. Before leaving, one of the men tries to illustrate the worthlessness of dreams by telling Santiago about his own dream. It concerns a treasure buried in an abandoned church in Spain where a sycamore tree grows. The church is the same one in which Santiago had his original dream, and he finally understands where his treasure is. He returns to Spain to find a chest of jewels and gold buried under the tree, and plans to return with it to Al-Fayoum, where he will reunite with Fatima, who awaits him.

CHARACTER LIST

Santiago   An adventurous young Andalusian shepherd determined to fulfill his Personal Legend, which is to find a treasure at the foot of the Egyptian pyramids. He is the book's protagonist.

The Alchemist   A 200-year-old, extremely powerful alchemist residing in the Al-Fayoum Oasis. He dresses in black, rides a white horse, and carries a scimitar, the Philosopher's Stone, and the Elixir of Life. He often speaks cryptically, but he understands the Soul of the World and the importance of Personal Legends.

Crystal Merchant   A struggling merchant who owns a crystal shop on top of a desolate hill. His shop was once popular but lost much of its business as Tangier lost its status as Egypt's premier port town. He is a good-hearted, devout Muslim, but has a crippling fear of change.

Englishman   A well-educated science student determined to learn the secrets of alchemy by learning from a true alchemist. He is a skeptic and loves reading his books.

Melchizedek   The King of Salem. He appears to possess magical powers and helps those pursuing their Personal Legends.

Fatima   A beautiful and chaste young "desert woman" who lives at the Al-Fayoum Oasis. She understands that she must allow Santiago to travel in pursuit of his dream.

Gypsy   An old woman living in Tarifa who interprets dreams. She reads palms and uses black-magic iconography, but she also keeps images of Christ.

Camel Driver A friendly former orchard owner and devout Muslim who feels content with his life despite losing his orchard in a flood. He has made the pilgrimage to Mecca and lives his life in service to omens from God.

The Tribal Chieftain of Al-Fayoum A strict and ruthless tribal chieftain who lives in luxury. He enforces Al-Fayoum's status as a neutral ground and believes in dreams and omens.

Merchant's daughter The beautiful and intelligent raven-haired daughter of the merchant who buys wool from Santiago.

The Monk A welcoming Coptic monk living in a monastery near the pyramids of Egypt.

Merchant A merchant who buys wool from Santiago on a yearly basis. He worries about being cheated so he demands that any wool he buys be sheared from the sheep in his presence.

Santiago's father A kindly, unadventurous family man who hoped Santiago would become a priest but gives him his blessing to become a shepherd.

Young Man A scam artist living in Tangier who speaks Arabic and Spanish.

Candy Seller A generous vendor in the Tangier marketplace who enjoys his occupation.

Barkeep A well-meaning bartender who lives in Tangier and speaks only Arabic.

Caravan Leader The bold leader of a caravan traveling across the Sahara Desert from Tangier to Egypt.

Analysis of Major Characters

Santiago

Santiago, a shepherd boy from a small Andalusian town, is the protagonist of *The Alchemist*. He is determined, headstrong, and curious to learn all he can about the world. As a result, he resisted his parent's desires that he become a priest and chose instead to work as a shepherd so that he would have the opportunity to travel throughout the country. Despite his natural adventurousness, Santiago remains conservative and self-satisfied in many ways until he dreams of uncovering a treasure hidden near the pyramids in Egypt. Santiago hesitates to pursue his dream until he meets Melchizedek, a mysterious old man who claims to be the king of Salem. After Melchizedek reveals to him the magical powers of nature, Santiago becomes a willing spiritual seeker and sets off to fulfill his Personal Legend, the innate dream each person has of accomplishing his or her greatest desire.

As the story progresses and Santiago comes closer to the treasure, he becomes more focused on his growing understanding of the mystical force that imbues everything, called the Soul of the World. The time he spends crossing the desert on his way to the pyramids teaches him to pay attention to the world around him and to see all of creation in his surroundings, even in a single grain of sand. The knowledge he gains from the desert allows him to recognize nature as a single, unified whole. His greatest spiritual advancement, however, comes after he meets the alchemist, who helps him to understand himself and to read the omens in his environment. Santiago ultimately learns to communicate with the wind and the sun and the Hand That Wrote All, a force evidently synonymous with God or Allah.

The Alchemist

Supposedly 200 years old, the alchemist is a mysterious character and an extremely powerful practitioner of alchemy who resides at the Al-Fayoum oasis. Many in Al-Fayoum do not know of his existence, and even the tribal chieftains must request an audience if they wish to see him. He has among his possessions the Master Work, considered the ultimate goal of alchemy, which consists of the Philosopher's Stone, capable of turning any metal into gold, and the Elixir of Life, able to cure all ills. In addition, he appears to possess magical powers. The alchemist mainly functions as a teacher to Santiago, though he often speaks in riddles and expects Santiago to learn more through experience than through verbal instruction.

The alchemist's teachings connect the book's dominant metaphor of alchemy—transforming one element into another more valuable element—to Santiago's own journey. The alchemist's wisdom connects him to the mystical Soul of the World. This connection provides him with his supernatural abilities, and it allows him to guide Santiago on his own quest to understand the Soul of the World. Santiago, with the alchemist's guidance, learns to read and communicate with the world around him, ultimately leading him to the treasure he seeks and to his own supernatural abilities. In other words, Santiago eventually undergoes his own transformation. The alchemist's hands-off method of teaching, however, suggests that no direct form of instruction can allow someone to connect with the Soul of the World. Instead, Santiago, and in fact any student, must teach and transform himself by listening to his own heart and to his environment.

THE CRYSTAL MERCHANT

The crystal merchant serves as an important friend to Santiago during Santiago's time in Tangier, but he also functions as a cautionary case of someone who has become complacent and given up the pursuit of his Personal Legend. He maintains a crystal shop on the top of a hill in Tangier and was rather successful until the city fell out of favor as a port. Although he is a good man who is devoutly religious and kind enough to take Santiago in, he fears pursuing his dream to make a pilgrimage to Mecca because he thinks he will have nothing to live for once he's achieved his dream. Although the crystal merchant feels rooted in his conservative approach to life, he takes no pride in it.

The crystal merchant is the most fully fleshed-out irredeemable character in *The Alchemist*. (The baker is another irredeemable character, as is Santiago's own father, but we don't see either of them as much as the crystal merchant). In other words, the novel portrays his fate as one to avoid, despite the fact that he comes across as a good person. The crystal merchant understands that he acts foolishly in not pursuing his Personal Legend, making it difficult to understand his motives when he refuses to change his ways, even after Santiago shows him the benefits of taking risks. Within the context of the story, he serves as an example of the dangers of an unfulfilled life, evident in his disappointment over his own life decisions.

MELCHIZEDEK

Melchizedek, who claims to be the King of Salem, appears to Santiago as an old man living in the Spanish town of Tarifa, and although he appears only briefly in the book, he plays an important role as he introduces several of the key concepts that we see repeated throughout *The Alchemist*. For example, he tells Santiago about Personal Legends, the Soul of the World, and Beginner's Luck. He also gives Santiago two magical stones, Urim and Thummim, which represent "yes" and "no," respectively, to help guide him on his journey. Melchizedek is also the first character in *The Alchemist* to display magical powers. Those powers help him convince Santiago to pursue his dream of finding a treasure near the pyramids in Egypt.

By his own account, Melchizedek plays a role in the lives of everyone who pursues his or her Personal Legend. He essentially motivates people to continue pursuing their Personal Legends in times of doubt, as he does when he meets Santiago in the novel. Although he appears to Santiago as a flesh-and-blood man, he explains that he appears to people more often as a symbol or idea. Evidently he has been serving this purpose for a long time, as he remembers helping the biblical Abraham in his own journey. Even when Melchizedek is not physically present, the magical stones he gives Santiago help Santiago to remain hopeful and focused as he pursues his Personal Legend.

THE ENGLISHMAN

The Englishman is a well-educated and ambitious aspiring alchemist. He is adventurous enough to join a caravan in search of the alchemist, but is rather anti-social. He prefers to read his large collection of books rather than interact with others or take interest in his surroundings. Because the Englishman and Santiago share a commitment to pursuing their Personal Legends, they quickly become friends. The Englishman, however, also challenges Santiago with his intellectual, knowledge-focused approach to life. He teaches Santiago the value of book learning and introduces him to important concepts in alchemy, such as the Master Work. But he must also learn from Santiago the importance of experience and friendship.

Because the Englishman focuses too much on his books, the alchemist believes he has not reached the point in his personal development that would allow him to be the alchemist's protégé. Using the Englishman as its example, the novel suggests that even though knowledge gained from books can be useful, one should not rely on it solely and unconditionally. True wisdom comes from experience, which one must earn through action.

FATIMA

The only female character in *The Alchemist* to get a modicum of attention, Fatima is defined by her beauty and her willingness to wait for Santiago while he pursues his Personal Legend. She lives at the Al-Fayoum oasis, where her primary duty in life consists of gathering water from the local well, and she says that, as a woman of the desert, she realizes that men must leave the women they love for long periods. When Santiago hesitates to leave Fatima and the oasis, she convinces him he must go. She has confidence that he will return if he loves her. Fatima says her ultimate goal is to love Santiago, and she appears to have no Personal Legend of her own.

THEMES, MOTIFS & SYMBOLS

THEMES

THE CENTRALITY OF PERSONAL LEGENDS

According to *The Alchemist,* Personal Legends serve as the only means by which an individual can live a satisfying life. In fact, the universe can only achieve perfection if all natural things continuously undergo a cycle of achieving their Personal Legends, evolving into higher beings with new Personal Legends, and then pursuing each new goal. This concept, that the individual pursuit of a Personal Legend exists as life's dominant—perhaps only—spiritual demand, lies at the center of the unique theology of *The Alchemist.* As we see when Santiago must give up his flock and leave Fatima, material success and even love pose obstacles to Santiago achieving his Personal Legend and must be delayed or ignored altogether. Those who do not pursue their Personal Legends, such as the crystal merchant, suffer regret and fail to experience the wealth and other favors that the universe bestows upon those who follow their Personal Legends. In the novel, even alchemy, the central symbol of the book, entails coaxing metal to achieve its own Personal Legend to turn into gold. As a result, the idea that all individuals should live in the singular pursuit of their individual dreams emerges as the primary theme of *The Alchemist.*

THE UNITY OF NATURE

In *The Alchemist,* the spiritual unity represented by the Soul of the World binds together all of nature, from human beings to desert sand. This idea underlies the parallel we see in the novel between the alchemist purifying metal into gold and Santiago purifying himself into someone capable of achieving his Personal Legend. According to the novel, the Soul of the World has created an ultimate desire, or Personal Legend, for everything, whether Santiago or a piece of iron. To accomplish its Personal Legend, each thing must learn to tap into the Soul of the World, which purifies it. That continual purification ultimately leads to perfection. This notion of humans, metals, and all other things sharing the same goal demonstrates that all elements in nature are essentially different forms of a single spirit.

Furthermore, over and over again we see that Santiago must communicate with nature in what the novel calls the common language of the world. Santiago's horse, for instance, communicates with him by showing him evidence of life in an apparently barren expanse of desert, and Santiago must employ the help of the desert, the wind, and the sun in order to turn into the wind. As the alchemist says when he leaves Santiago, everything from a grain of sand to God himself shares the same spiritual essence. This pantheistic view dominates *The Alchemist,* and along with the individual, evolutionary theology expressed in the theme of alchemy, it forms the book's core spiritual message.

THE DANGER OF FEAR
Fear persistently comes up throughout Santiago's journey as the primary obstacle to Santiago's successful achievement of his Personal Legend. Santiago experiences several forms of fear: a childhood fear of having the gypsy woman interpret his dream; a material fear of losing his wealth by departing to Tangier or by joining the desert caravan; the physical fear of dying in the battle at Al-Fayoum; and the spiritual fear that he will fail to turn himself into the wind when the alchemist forces him to try.

Santiago's mentors, from Melchizedek to the alchemist, condemn fear by comparing it to materialism, and they describe it as a product of misunderstanding how the universe treats those pursuing their Personal Legends. Fear, they suggest, should become irrelevant, even in the face of death, if one faithfully pursues one's dreams.

Just as those who disregard fear appear as enlightened figures, fear dominates *The Alchemist's* weakest characters. The crystal merchant in particular represents someone who has allowed fear to rule his life. Although he wants to make the pilgrimage to Mecca required of every Muslim, he fears that once he's made the trip he will have nothing else to live for. As a result, he remains deeply unhappy, reinforcing the notion that fear acts as an obstacle to a happy and fulfilled life.

MOTIFS

DREAMS
In *The Alchemist,* dreams represent not only an outlet into one's inner desires, but also a form of communication with the Soul of the

World. Santiago's dream of a treasure in Egypt, for instance, reveals to him his Personal Legend and sets the entire plot of the Alchemist in motion. Whether or not an individual believes in dreams creates a dividing line between the "enlightened" and "unenlightened" characters in the novel. The tribal chieftain takes Santiago's dream of the hawks very seriously and he understands the dream as a message from the desert of an impending assault. He also relates a story about the biblical Joseph's ability to read dreams, concluding that those who truly believe in dreams also have the ability to read them. The chief's insight, we see, allows him to successfully defend the oasis against attack. Later in the novel, the man who beats Santiago does not believe in his own dream, but when he describes it to Santiago, Santiago recognizes it as an omen telling him where to find the treasure. The importance of actual, sleeping dreams parallels the importance of personal, symbolic dreams as embodied by Personal Legends.

MAKTUB

Many of the characters that Santiago meets during his journey use the word *maktub*, which as the crystal merchant explains, means "it is written." The word typically appears just as Santiago is about to turn to a new chapter in his quest, usually by taking a big risk or abandoning a comfortable situation. It becomes a reassuring refrain for Santiago, because it reminds him to see his actions in the context of fate. As Santiago learns, fate always cooperates with those in pursuit of their Personal Legends, so as long as he remains focused on his goal he can find comfort in the fact that his destiny has already been written in the history of the world. In addition, the repetition of *maktub* reinforces the biblical tone of *The Alchemist*. The word gives Santiago's story the universality and spiritual heft of a parable or myth (much like the other capitalized terms that dominate the book, such as *the Soul of the World* and *the Hand that Wrote All*).

OMENS

The motif of omens serves a dual purpose in *The Alchemist*. For one, omens offer Santiago guidance on his journey and reassure him that the Soul of the World has endorsed his journey. As Melchizedek explains, omens make up part of the Universal Language of the World, and if Santiago taps into this language he can always find the meaning in his environment. For example, when the Urim and Thummim drop from Santiago's pocket, Santiago chooses to consider the event an omen. In doing so, he continues to feel that the

MOTIFS

universe conspires to help him, and he finds meaning in the seemingly random event. In this way, the motif of omens reinforces the book's theme of the unity of nature.

Omens also serve to demonstrate Santiago's spiritual growth throughout the story. The omens that Santiago experiences grow in relevance from being small, limited events to important visions that affect many lives. The vision of the hawks and approaching armies that Santiago has in Al-Fayoum, for example, tells him of an assault on the oasis that could lead to the death of hundreds. That his omens become more and more important signifies that Santiago is getting closer to understanding the pure Language of the World.

Symbols

Santiago's Sheep

Santiago's sheep symbolize the sort of existence lived by those who are completely blind to their Personal Legends. Santiago loves his sheep, but he also expresses thinly veiled disrespect for them because of their animal desire for mere food and water. He thinks that his sheep do not appreciate all the wonderful lands that Santiago discovers during his travels. Also, in a disturbing image, he imagines that his sheep are so blindly trusting that he could kill them one by one without their noticing. These sheep symbolize the characters in the book like the baker and the crystal merchant, who do not pursue their Personal Legends. Like the sheep, these characters content themselves with their material desires and social acceptance. Accordingly, they lose the ability to appreciate certain aspects of creation and tend to miss out on many opportunities because of their limited perspective.

Alchemy

Alchemy, in which a base metal is transformed into a more valuable metal like gold, functions as the dominant symbol in *The Alchemist* and represents Santiago's journey to achieve his Personal Legend. The symbol also gives the novel its title. *The Alchemist* describes the process of turning base metal into gold as equivalent to the base metal realizing its Personal Legend. In the parlance of the book, the metal must rid itself of all impurities to achieve a higher evolutionary state. Similarly, Santiago must rid himself of impurities, such as his desire for his parents' acceptance, his desire to live as a rich shepherd, and even his desire to live with Fatima, in order to realize his own Personal Legend and achieve a higher state. The way a person learns the craft of alchemy parallels the way in which a person achieves his Personal Legend. As the alchemist tells Santiago, although many tomes have been written about alchemy, these books only complicate the craft. In fact, all the secrets of alchemy exist on the small Emerald Tablet, and these secrets cannot be expressed in words. Likewise, no written instructions can guide a person to his Personal Legend. The person must follow his own instincts and the omens provided by the Soul of the World. The alchemist chooses Santiago as his pupil rather than the Englishman largely because Santiago does not depend on books and reason to understand the world. By listening to the Soul of the World, Santiago ultimately enters into communion with all of nature, including the wind and the sun, and he reaches a higher state of being.

THE DESERT

The desert, with its harsh conditions and tribal wars, symbolizes the serious difficulties that await anyone in pursuit of his or her Personal Legend, but it also serves as an important teacher to Santiago during his journey to the pyramids. As the alchemist puts it, tests are an inherent part of all Personal Legends, because they are necessary to create spiritual growth. More than the desert heat, the desert's silence, emptiness, and monotony test Santiago. As Santiago learns, however, even the desert, despite appearing barren, contains life and the Soul of the World. Santiago begins to understand his environment and to see the signs of life in what seems to be a wasteland. Eventually he learns to recognize all of creation in a single grain of sand, and in the greatest test he faces during the book, he finds he is able to enlist the desert in his effort to become the wind.

Summary & Analysis

Part One, Section 1

Summary: Prologue

The alchemist reads a book containing the story of Narcissus. According to legend, Narcissus kneeled every day beside a lake to admire his reflection, until one day he became so fascinated with his own beauty that he fell into the lake and drowned. The goddess of the forest appeared at the lake and found the water transformed into salty tears. She asked the lake why it cried for Narcissus, assuming it had admired Narcissus's beauty. The lake replies that it was enjoying its own beauty reflected in Narcissus's eyes.

Summary: Section One

The third-person narrator describes a shepherd named Santiago arriving with his flock at an abandoned church. Santiago decides to sleep there. A giant sycamore tree grows in the spot where a sacristy once stood. While Santiago sleeps, he has a disturbing dream (we do not learn exactly what the dream was). When he wakes, his flock begins to stir, and Santiago talks to the sheep about a girl he met the year prior. She is the daughter of a merchant who Santiago is visiting to sell some wool.

When Santiago arrives, the merchant asks him to wait until afternoon to sell him wool. While Santiago reads, he meets the merchant's daughter and talks to her about life in the village. She asks why he chooses to be a shepherd even though he can read. Santiago avoids the question, preferring instead to talk about his travels. Santiago finds the merchant's daughter's Moorish eyes and raven-colored hair entrancing. He experiences for the first time a desire to stay in one place for the rest of his life. When the merchant finally appears, he asks Santiago for the wool of four sheep and tells him to return the next year.

The story jumps forward in time almost a year, to four days before Santiago's next visit to the village. He stays in the abandoned church and daydreams about the merchant's daughter. As he urges his sheep along, he admires their loyalty. Santiago imagines he could kill his sheep one by one, and each one would be none the wiser. He feels troubled by his thought, and that night has the same troubling dream he had the year before.

Santiago recalls the day he told his father he wanted to travel instead of becoming a priest. His father told him that travelers see other lands, but do not change as a result. They just end up being nostalgic for the past. His father said the only people of their class who travel are shepherds. The next day, Santiago's father gave him three gold coins to purchase a flock of sheep. He encouraged Santiago to travel, but said Santiago would learn that their own countryside was best. As he recalls the scene, Santiago senses that his father also would have liked to travel, but could not afford to while raising a family. Santiago wonders if his sheep enjoy discovering new roads and sights each day, but decides they only care about eating. He compares the flock's singlemindedness to his own preoccupation with the merchant's daughter. Suddenly, Santiago remembers that an old woman in the nearby village of Tarifa interprets dreams. He decides to visit her.

ANALYSIS

The prologue of the Alchemist runs only a little more than one page, but it gives the reader several clues about what to expect in the story. The alchemist says the book containing the story of Narcissus belonged to someone in "the caravan," hinting that a journey may occur during the course of the tale. The alchemist also expresses surprise that the author of the book extended the popular legend of Narcissus past its traditional conclusion. The usual version of the legend ends as Narcissus dies looking into a lake, illustrating the danger of vanity. In the version Santiago reads, however, we learn that the lake felt upset that Narcissus had drowned, because it enjoyed feeding its own vanity while looking into Narcissus's eyes. This idea that vanity can serve a good cause despite its perils will become an important theme of the book. The Narcissus story also readies the reader for the magical, mythic quality of *The Alchemist*. It introduces us to a world where a lake can speak, goddesses roam the countryside, and magic is a fact of life.

Almost as soon as we meet Santiago, we learn that he is not an ordinary shepherd. Most notably, he reads regularly, which surprises the merchant's daughter. Shepherding presents an unusual career path for an educated young man, but Santiago clearly feels comfortable with his choice. We also see that Santiago's bearing has quickly made him successful at his job. He has regular customers, purchases books as he pleases, and appears to be content with his lifestyle. Only his attraction to the merchant's daughter, who the narrator says acts as the first signal that Santiago's life will never be the same, makes him question his choice to be a traveling shepherd. The other signal is Santiago's troubling dream, which is not initially explained but always occurs while he sleeps under the sycamore tree growing in the sacristy of the abandoned church. This mysterious dream repeats in two consecutive passages a year apart, and it serves as an important piece of foreshadowing.

Santiago enjoys his life as a shepherd not only because it allows him to travel, but also because he loves his sheep. Santiago notices his flock's ability to find contentment through food and water alone, and he almost envies the fact that they never have to make any decisions. Happiness for a human being, he thinks, seems much more complicated. On the other hand, Santiago feels frustrated by the fact that his sheep can't share his appreciation of travel. He imagines that he could kill his sheep one by one and the flock would not even notice. The unexpectedly violent image shows us that the sheep live blind to important truths and that they are not to be emulated. Santiago wonders if all humans are like his sheep: looking only for physical contentment and living without ever appreciating life. Later, this tension becomes very important to Santiago: even though he has traveled throughout Spain, he still feels limited. He wonders if his relatively local travels, comforting stacks of books, and obedient flock play the same role in his life that food and water play in the lives of his sheep. Santiago's thoughts imply that he must seek out a higher purpose if he wants to be truly happy.

SECTION 2

SUMMARY

Upon meeting Santiago, the dream interpreter takes his hands and begins chanting a Gypsy prayer. When he was a boy, Santiago feared being captured by Gypsies, and he worries the fear will return. He takes solace in an image of Jesus in the room, but his hands still tremble. When Santiago realizes that the dream interpreter detects his nervousness, he pulls his hands away and says he doesn't want a palm reading. The dream interpreter replies that she can help him and that she will still charge him if he leaves early. Santiago decides to go ahead and learn the meaning of his dream.

In his dream, Santiago is in a field with his sheep when a child starts to play with them. The child grabs Santiago's hands, transports him to the pyramids in Egypt, and tells him that he will find a treasure near them. As the child begins to say the exact location of the treasure, Santiago wakes up.

After listening to the dream, the dream interpreter says she will not charge him for her service, but that she wants ten percent of the treasure when he finds it. Santiago laughs in disbelief and agrees to swear that he will share his treasure. Then the dream interpreter goes on to insist that Santiago travel to the pyramids and find the treasure. She says that she knows the treasure really exists because it was a child who pointed it out in the dream. Skeptical, Santiago leaves, disappointed but relieved he didn't have to pay anything.

Santiago eats and buys a new book in Tarifa. He rests in town to wait out the hot sun before he moves on. He is reading when an old man who resembles an Arab approaches him. Santiago ignores the man initially, but the old man persistently questions Santiago about the book until Santiago relents and talks to him. To Santiago's surprise, the old man knows the book. The old man says it is the same as most other books, because it describes how people end up believing "the world's greatest lie," that nobody can choose his own fate, or "Personal Legend." Santiago says he controlled his destiny by becoming a shepherd instead of a priest.

During their conversation, the old man introduces himself as Melchizedek and says he is the King of Salem. Santiago has never heard of Salem and thinks the old man is crazy. The old man says that if Santiago gives him one tenth of his sheep, he will tell him how to find the hidden treasure. Santiago guesses the old man works with the dream interpreter in a Gypsy scam, since in no other way could he have known about the treasure. Melchizedek then proceeds to write the names of Santiago's mother and father in the sand with a nearby stick—names Santiago never told the Gypsy.

ANALYSIS

The first section of *The Alchemist* introduces Santiago as a happy and successful, if somewhat complacent, young shepherd. He does his job well, feels satisfied with his choices, and maintains a youthful crush on a local girl with exotic features. To Santiago, his life seems unique and barrier-breaking. In this section, however, he begins to feel that a whole world exists that he has not seen, and though Santiago may be something of an adventurer compared to his parents and the people around him, he may still resemble his sheep. During his meetings with the Gypsy and Melchizedek, Santiago glimpses possibilities for his life that he had never considered, and the reader has some early hints that Santiago will have to choose between remaining a relatively adventurous Spanish shepherd and breaking out of his comfort zone to pursue his Personal Legend.

The occult imagery associated with the Gypsy dream interpreter who engages in palm reading serves as the initial indication that Santiago enters into uncharted territory. The Gypsy also keeps an image of Christ, which suggests that all faiths are connected, but Santiago's hands still tremble. Upon relating his dream of being shown a treasure at the pyramids, Santiago feels shocked when the Gypsy tells him to make the pilgrimage to Egypt. When he leaves, Santiago dismisses the incident and believes he got away easily by promising the Gypsy one tenth of a supposed treasure that may not even exist. The encounter shows that Santiago does not yet place any importance on his dreams. He may have chosen to be a shepherd instead of a priest, but traveling all the way to Egypt in search of treasure because of a dream remains beyond Santiago's scope. Instead, he immediately goes back to the life he knows. He gets a new book, drinks some wine, and thinks about the merchant's daughter.

Melchizedek, the old man Santiago meets, provides the push Santiago needs to convince him to pursue his dream. Initially, Santiago has no interest in Melchizedek, but Melchizedek gets Santiago's attention by saying he knows the book Santiago is reading. Santiago perks up, possibly because he senses a kindred spirit in his fellow reader. Melchizedek says Santiago's book demonstrates the world's greatest lie: that fate controls our lives more than we do. Santiago feels he understands Melchizedek's point. After all, he chose his own path and became a shepherd. Still, Santiago suspects a Gypsy scam when Melchizedek, who calls himself the King of Salem, speaks knowingly of Santiago's dream and demands some of his sheep in return for a clue about the treasure. But Melchizedek begins to change Santiago's mind when he reveals that he knows the names of Santiago's parents, the seminary he attended, and other things that Santiago hadn't told to anyone, demonstrating that he has a supernatural ability. Persuaded that Melchizedek is at least wise, if not an actual king, Santiago feels convinced that he should listen to Melichizedek.

Section 3

Summary

Melchizedek explains the concept of the Personal Legend to Santiago. A person's Personal Legend, he says, represents what that person most desires to accomplish in his or her life. Everyone knows their Personal Legend when they are young, but as time passes, a mysterious force makes them feel they will never achieve their Personal Legend.

Melchizedek asks Santiago why he lives as a shepherd. When Santiago says he likes to travel, Melchizedek points to a baker working nearby. The baker likes to travel, but became a baker because people consider them more important than shepherds. Melchizedek worries that Santiago is about to give up on his own Personal Legend and says he appears to everyone who is about to quit pursuing his or her dream. He usually appears as a solution to a problem or an idea and once appeared as an emerald to a miner. He says he will help Santiago if Santiago hands over one-tenth of his flock.

The meeting upsets Santiago, and he begins wandering through the city. He buys bread from the baker Melchizedek mentioned. He then stops at a booth selling tickets for the boat to Africa, but decides to remain a shepherd. Then, an intense wind, called the *levanter*, picks up. Santiago envies the wind's freedom, and decides the merchant's daughter and his sheep are only steps on the way toward his Personal Legend.

Santiago finds Melchizedek the next day and brings six sheep. He tells Melchizedek he sold the rest of his sheep the day before. Melchizedek says Santiago can find his treasure in Egypt by the pyramids. Initially, Santiago feels annoyed that Melchizedek does not give a more exact location, but then a butterfly appears. Melchizedek explains the butterfly is Santiago's first omen and opens his cape to reveal a jeweled breastplate. Melchizedek gives Santiago two stones from the breastplate. He says the stones are called Urim and Thummim and they represent "yes" and "no." They will help Santiago to read omens.

Before Melchizedek leaves, he tells Santiago the story of a shopkeeper who sends his son to learn the secret of happiness from the wisest man in the world. The boy finds the man in a beautiful castle in the desert. The wise man tells the boy to spend time looking around while balancing a spoonful of oil. When the boy returns, he says he didn't pay attention to any of the castle's splendor because he concentrated on the oil. The wise man sends him out again to see the castle, and the boy returns having seen the castle but having also spilled the oil. The wise man tells him he must admire the castle without forgetting the oil. The story reminds Santiago of a shepherd always needing to remember his flock.

As Melchizedek watches Santiago's ship pull out of port toward Africa, he remembers making the same bargain with Abraham that he made with Santiago.

ANALYSIS

Santiago's meeting with Melchizedek, which teaches him about Personal Legends and their importance to anyone who wants to live a fulfilling life, essentially marks the point when Santiago decides to embark on his journey to Egypt. Subsequently, the book's plot largely focuses on Santiago following his dream and trying to live out his Personal Legend. *The Alchemist* subsequently resembles other "follow your dream narratives," though Melchizedek's lesson differs from the lessons in those narratives in a few important ways. For one, Melchizedek insists that everyone knows their Personal Legend when they are young. Personal Legends do not become clear to people only later in life. In addition, the baker's story illustrates that society works as an enemy of Personal Legends. When the baker adopts society's traditional expectations of success, he forgets his true Personal Legend. But as Melchizedek explains, the force that age and society exert against anyone pursuing their Personal Legend plays a vital role in preparing that person to achieve her or his goal.

Santiago's sheep exemplify the ways in which material possessions can help or hinder a person in his quest to reach his Personal Legend. Without his flock, for instance, Santiago would not have had anything to trade with Melchizedek to get the clue about the next step in his Personal Legend. On the other hand, Santiago's flock provided him with material wealth and personal satisfaction, both of which tempted him to disregard his Personal Legend and remain in Spain. When Santiago watches the strong levanter wind, he realizes that he must move freely as well. Once Santiago recognizes his flock as just one step in a quest toward an ultimate goal, as opposed to an end in and of itself, he becomes as free as the wind. This realization, that one must be free to move and develop without remaining tied down by material possessions, as well as the image of wind, will resurface several times as the story progresses.

Coelho employs several stylistic strategies in this section that give *The Alchemist* a mythic quality. He introduces phrases and concepts such as The Soul of the World, the Personal Legend, and the Warriors of the Light, which continue to appear throughout the book. These phrases resonate by their repetition and because they often appear in capital letters. By echoing biblical and Koranic phrases, such as the Lamb of God or Inshallah ("if Allah wills"), they make *The Alchemist* resemble a spiritual text. They also give the reader a sense of a higher power guiding the material world we see. Another strategy Coelho uses to give the book a mythic tone involves using stories as moral lessons. Specifically, Melchizedek's stories of the baker, the miner, and shopkeeper's son recall moral allegories in spiritual texts. As a result, the novel comes across as a parable, more akin to the Bible or Koran than a work of realism.

Section 4

Summary

Santiago arrives in Tangier and sits at a bar. When he sees people engaging in local behaviors such as sharing pipes and walking hand-in-hand, he scorns the people as infidels. He worries that he can't speak Arabic, reassuring himself only with the money in his pouch. A man of similar age and appearance as Santiago addresses him in Spanish. Santiago tells him he needs to get to the pyramids and offers to pay him to serve as a guide. The young man explains that the route across the Sahara Desert is dangerous, and Santiago needs to show that he has enough money to make the trip. The bar owner speaks angrily to the young man in Arabic, and the young man drags Santiago outside, saying the bar owner is a thief. Santiago gives the young man his money to purchase camels.

The two traverse a crowded marketplace and Santiago notices a sword on display. Santiago asks the young man to find out the sword's price, but soon realizes the young man has disappeared. Santiago waits at the marketplace until nightfall for the young man to return and begins to cry when he realizes he's been robbed. Santiago takes inventory of his remaining possessions. He has his book, his jacket, and the stones Melchizedek gave him. He considers selling the stones to pay for a trip back home. He asks the stones if he will find his treasure, but when he puts his hand in his pocket he realizes the stones have slipped through a hole and fallen to the ground. As he collects them, he remembers his promise to make his own decisions, and he resolves to continue his mission.

Santiago falls asleep in the marketplace. He wakes as merchants begin setting up shop for the day. A candy seller offers Santiago his first sweet. Santiago notices that some merchants speak Spanish and others speak Arabic, but they communicate with each other without words. Meanwhile, a crystal merchant wakes up feeling anxious. For thirty years, his shop has stood on a desolate street and attracted few customers. Business once boomed when Tangier was a busy port, but sales have fallen off ever since nearby Ceuta became a more important town.

That day, the crystal merchant sees Santiago looking around his shop. Santiago offers to clean glasses in the shop window in exchange for food, but the crystal merchant does not respond. Santiago cleans the glasses anyway. During that time, two customers enter and buy crystal. When Santiago finishes, the crystal merchant takes him to a café. He explains that Santiago didn't need to clean, because the Koran orders him to feed the hungry. Santiago replies that they both needed to cleanse their minds of bad thoughts. The crystal merchant says it was a good omen that customers entered while Santiago cleaned and offers Santiago a job. Santiago says he will clean all the merchant's crystal overnight in exchange for money to get to Egypt. The merchant replies that the trip to Egypt is so long and expensive that Santiago couldn't earn enough for the trip in a year. Santiago feels disappointed but agrees to take the job.

ANALYSIS

Santiago's initial experience in Tangier illustrates the fact that moving on from a comfortable situation can present a challenge, even if the challenge arises in the pursuit of a Personal Legend. As soon as Santiago arrives in Tangier, he feels suspicious of the "infidel" Muslims. Tangier seems uncomfortably foreign, largely because the people behave differently in Spain, and Santiago dislikes the place. Santiago quickly pays for these prejudices when he decides to trust the familiar, Spanish-speaking young man instead of the Arabic-speaking bartender. When the young man robs Santiago, Santiago realizes that he must readjust his perspective on his surroundings. Notably, Santiago lost track of the young man while admiring a sword that he planned to buy upon the young man's return. By focusing on a material possession instead of his Personal Legend, Santiago lost the only wealth he had. At nightfall, Santiago laments all of his lost material possessions. He only remembers his quest when he feels Urim and Thummim and appreciates them for their symbolic value rather than their material value. Remembering the stones and Melchizedek's words immediately renews Santiago's commitment to his quest.

We see in the crystal merchant, as with the baker, someone who has forgotten his Personal Legend and become trapped in an adequate, but unfulfilling, situation. He has not adapted to Tangier becoming a less vibrant port town because he feels scared of change. The crystal merchant's belief in omens presents his most redeeming trait. From the very first moment he sees Santiago, he decides to stop and watch him even though Santiago clearly has no money. The crystal merchant proceeds to offer Santiago a job, despite the fact that his business already struggles, because he considers as omens the visitors who arrived while Santiago cleaned. Throughout *The Alchemist,* characters who believe in omens appear wise and prosper. Unlike materialistic characters, these characters accept the interconnectedness of Personal Legends and The Soul of the World. We also see this interconnectedness in Santiago's run-in with the candy seller and the other merchants, who communicate in a "universal language" despite the fact that the actual languages they speak differ.

From this section forward, the book no longer refers to Santiago by name. Instead, the novel refers to him only as "the boy." The change has two effects. First, it allows the reader to experience Santiago as a mysterious stranger, as the crystal merchant and other people who encounter Santiago see him. Second, it turns Santiago into a universal symbol rather than an individual character. Referring to Santiago as "the boy" makes him a mythic figure, just as Melchizedek attains mythic significance when Santiago forgets his name and starts thinking of him as "the old man." In turn, *The Alchemist* acts less as a personal story about the adventures of one character and more as an allegory with universal implications. This change raises the question of why Santiago ever had a name in the first place. Although no single answer emerges, it may be that readers can better identify with Santiago when he has a name and identity. Once the reader has achieved that level of sympathy, his name is no longer necessary.

PART TWO, SECTION 5

SUMMARY

After almost a month of work, Santiago feels annoyed with his new job. The crystal merchant is grouchy and the work is tedious. The job pays decently, but Santiago would still need a year's savings to afford a new flock of sheep. Santiago offers to build a display case to place outside the shop and attract more customers, but the crystal merchant fears people will bump into it and break crystals. He argues that business has been good and asks why Santiago wants more. Santiago says he needs to follow his Personal Legend and go to the pyramids.

The crystal merchant doesn't understand why Santiago feels so determined. He warns that the display case could be a mistake just as easily as it could help them make more money. The crystal merchant says he lives by the Koran, which makes few demands, but as he explains these demands he recalls that one of them is a pilgrimage to Mecca. Traveling to Mecca has long been his dream. Santiago asks why he has never made the trip, and the merchant says that if he did, he would no longer have anything to live for. He prefers to have his dream. In recognition of Santiago's dream, he agrees to build the display case.

The display case increases customer traffic, and Santiago realizes that, within six months, he will have enough to return to Tarifa and buy twice as many sheep as he originally owned. After hearing a man complain about the lack of places to drink on the hill, Santiago suggests that the crystal merchant also sell tea in crystal glasses. The crystal merchant hesitates to enter a new business, but he invites Santiago to smoke a pipe with him to discuss the idea. He tells Santiago he has become aware of the danger of ignoring blessings, and agrees to sell tea. The tea becomes popular, and the crystal merchant hires more employees as his business increases.

The months pass and Santiago, nearly a year after his arrival in Africa, has become rich as a result of the crystal shop's success. One morning, Santiago wakes early. He tells the crystal merchant he wants to return to Tarifa and buy a large flock of sheep, and he encourages the crystal merchant to travel to Mecca. The crystal merchant says he will not go to Mecca and Santiago will not go home. Santiago asks how he knows, and the crystal merchant says "*maktub*," which means "it is written."

As Santiago packs, the two stones, Urim and Thummim, fall to the floor, reminding Santiago of Melchizedek. He considers how much he has achieved by traveling to Tangier and reconsiders returning home and becoming a shepherd again. The trip through the desert to the pyramids will offer him the chance to get to know a new place, and he can always return to his sheep. He decides to continue pursuing his Personal Legend, and visits a supplier for desert caravans.

ANALYSIS

Santiago and the crystal merchant represent the different paths people may choose in life, with fear and complacency acting as the dividing factors between the courses they select. Whereas Santiago feels eager to pursue his Personal Legend and get to Egypt, the crystal merchant fears pursuing his own dream to make a pilgrimage to Mecca because he worries he will have nothing to live for afterward. He also feels comfortable with what he has and does not seek out more. Santiago has already faced several setbacks in his own quest, but they have all been due to outside forces, such as the thief who robbed him. The crystal merchant faces none of these difficulties. Rather, he has made a personal decision to avoid his dream because of his own fear and complacency. Although Santiago will continue to face many more material setbacks in pursuit of his Personal Legend, these factors remain the most difficult obstacles for him to overcome.

Santiago shows the crystal merchant that by ignoring his greater dreams he also reduces his perspective, to the point that his day-to-day business suffers. The crystal merchant displays the same sense of wariness about traveling to Mecca that he displayed when Santiago proposed that they build a crystal stand or sell tea. When the crystal merchant finally agrees to risk changing his business, which could affect his lifestyle, his business thrives. Santiago compares his experience with the crystal merchant to his own experience with his sheep. Although Santiago learned some facts from his sheep, he could never have learned Arabic from them. He concludes that sometimes you need to abandon a comfortable lifestyle in order to grow. Notably, the crystal merchant becomes depressed after his success with Santiago. When the crystal merchant realizes that the possibilities for his life have no limits, he feels weak and lazy for having resisted his dreams.

Despite the lessons Santiago learns while working for the crystal merchant, he initially decides to use his earnings to buy a new flock of sheep and return to his old life. He must consult Urim and Thummim once more in order to renew his commitment to his goal. Santiago realizes that although the prospect of returning to the comfort of his sheep tempts him, had he not continued in pursuit of his Personal Legend when he first arrived in Tangier, he never would have found success with the crystal merchant. Urim and Thummim and the memory of Melchizedek remind him that a much greater goal exists than just a comfortable life. This epiphany allows Santiago to happily and confidently face his impending trip across the desert. The crystal merchant, meanwhile, does not feel surprised at Santiago's departure. He invokes a term repeated throughout the book—*maktub,* which means "it is written"—suggesting that Santiago has a destiny to fulfill. This emphasis on the importance of fate becomes only more prominent as Santiago continues to search for his treasure.

SECTION 6

SUMMARY

An Englishman sits in a stable preparing for a caravan trip through the Sahara Desert. He studies alchemy and hopes to learn from an alchemist residing in the desert's Al-Fayoum oasis. The legendary alchemist supposedly discovered the Philosopher's Stone and the Elixir of Life.

Santiago also joins the group traveling with the desert caravan, and he tells the Englishman his story of working for the crystal merchant. The Englishman seems unfriendly at first, telling Santiago that Urim and Thummim are cheap rock crystals. Santiago explains that a king gave them to him, but that the Englishman wouldn't understand. The Englishman says he does understand, because he read the story of the Urim and Thummim in the Bible. He explains that he is seeking an alchemist, and Santiago replies that he is heading to Egypt to look for treasure. As the caravan sets off, the caravan leader orders everyone to swear to their God that they will follow his orders. The Englishman reads constantly, so Santiago speaks to him very little during the journey. Instead, he daydreams, tries to read his book, and befriends a camel driver.

Santiago relates his adventures as a shepherd to the camel driver, and one day the camel driver tells Santiago his own story.

He maintained a successful orchard, had traveled to Mecca, and felt he could die happy. However, one day an earthquake caused a flood that ruined his land, so he had to become a camel driver. These events taught him not to fear losing material possessions.

The caravan runs into groups of hooded Bedouins who warn of nearby thieves, barbarians, and tribal wars. The caravan travels quickly through the dangerous area, and no one speaks at night. The travelers do not light their fires either, so as not to draw attention, and they must huddle around a circle of camels to stay warm. One night, the Englishman, unable to sleep, walks with Santiago around the encampment. Santiago goes into detail about the story of his life, and the Englishman compares Santiago's success to the governing principle of alchemy, called the Soul of the World. The term refers to the positive force of the world that works for the betterment of all things, both living and inanimate.

Santiago decides to learn more about the Soul of the World by reading the Englishman's alchemy books. He learns that the most important text in alchemy is inscribed on an emerald, called the Emerald Tablet, and runs only a few lines. He also reads about the Master Work, which entails purifying metals to the point that all that is left of them is the Soul of the World. The Master Work has two parts, a liquid part called the Elixir of Life that cures all ills, and a solid part called the Philosopher's Stone that can transform any metal into gold. The Englishman talks to Santiago about alchemy but feels disappointed with his superficial understanding of the practice.

A war begins in the desert but the caravan reaches the oasis safely. Egypt remains a long distance away, but Santiago feels pleased not to travel in fear any longer.

ANALYSIS

We finally have an indication of why the book is titled *The Alchemist* when we meet the Englishman, who is traveling to meet the alchemist in the desert. The Englishman serves as both a friend and a foil to Santiago during their time together. He represents a world view we haven't seen before in the novel: a highly educated Westerner who relies on learning rather than instinct to guide him. Santiago initially bonds with the Englishman, but a major tension exists between the two. Whereas Santiago likes to bask in the experience of the desert and speak to his companions in the caravan, the Englishman loses himself in his books. Though Santiago

SUMMARY & ANALYSIS

and the Englishman try to learn from each other's preoccupations, Santiago by reading about alchemy and the Englishman by observing the desert, each ultimately decides that his own approach to life is the superior one.

The Englishman also plays a vital role in the novel in that he introduces Santiago to the practice of alchemy. The terms and concepts that Santiago learns in the Englishman's alchemy books represent some of the most important metaphors in the book. Just as Santiago must purify himself from material concerns and external pressures in order to focus on his Personal Legend, alchemists seek to rid metals of impurities in order to reveal the Soul of the World. Also, just as some alchemists study for years to learn something that can be written in just a few lines on the Emerald Tablet, Santiago's quest for his Personal Legend appears complex and difficult but is quite simple in reality. The analogy between finding the Soul of the World in a metal and finding the Soul of the World through a personal mission to live out one's Personal Legend becomes more apparent and important as the story continues.

The fact that the novel compares the refinement of metals and humans also has significance. In *The Alchemist,* one mystical force connects everything, linking people even to inanimate objects and elements like gold or other metals. Moreover, Santiago's Personal Legend centers on finding not just a metaphorical treasure, but an actual treasure. Although he gives up his wealth (his sheep, specifically) for his quest when he sets out, he does so in hopes of finding even more wealth, just as a base metal becomes a more valuable metal through alchemy. We also see over and over in the book that those willing to pursue their Personal Legends enjoy material success in addition to feeling more satisfied with their lives. This arguably materialistic conceit, in which material wealth and spiritual purity go hand-in-hand, sets the belief system of *The Alchemist* apart from many traditional spiritual belief systems.

Santiago finds a kindred spirit in the camel driver. Much like the crystal merchant, the camel driver devotes himself to Islam and has a strong belief in the world's interconnectedness. Unlike the crystal merchant, however, he has overcome his complacency. At one point, he lived a life much like that of the crystal merchant. He worked as a gardener and had even made the trip to Mecca that the crystal merchant dreams of. He felt content and prepared to die, until an earthquake and flood wiped out his orchard. While difficult, the lesson taught him the importance of overcoming his fear of the unknown and moving forward. The camel driver also invokes the word *maktub* to stress the inevitability of fate, and his overriding belief in the interconnectedness of the world frees him from the caravan's fear of the tribal wars. As he believes, anything that happens is meant to happen, including his own death.

SECTION 7

SUMMARY

The alchemist watches from Al-Fayoum as the caravan arrives. The village around Al-Fayoum buzzes with excitement, but the alchemist has seen many people come and go so he pays no attention. Omens have made the alchemist aware that someone traveling with the caravan will learn from him, and the alchemist wonders how capable his new apprentice will be.

Al-Fayoum, a desert oasis, amazes Santiago. The place appears larger than many Spanish towns. Curious children crowd the caravan and women accost the caravan's merchants. The camel driver tells Santiago that they are safe in Al-Fayoum. Warring tribes avoid it because mostly women and children inhabit the place. The caravan leader explains that the group will remain in Al-Fayoum until the war ends, and that they must hand over their arms and stay in tents with locals and fellow travelers. Santiago sleeps in a tent with five other young men his age. The next morning, he regales his roommates with stories of his life as a shepherd in Spain, but the Englishman interrupts him to ask for help finding the alchemist.

The pair searches all day for the alchemist's tent without luck. Santiago asks an old man about the alchemist, and the old man replies that even tribal chieftains can't meet with the alchemist. Santiago decides to ask one more person before giving up, and approaches a young woman at a well. As soon as he sees her, he falls deeply in love with her. The girl introduces herself as Fatima and explains that the alchemist communicates with desert spirits and lives in the south of Al-Fayoum. The Englishman disappears to pursue the alchemist, and Fatima leaves after getting water. Santiago remains where he stands, love-struck.

The next day, Santiago returns to the well, hoping to see Fatima again. He finds the Englishman there as well. The Englishman explains he waited all day for the alchemist. When the alchemist finally arrived, the Englishman asked how to turn lead into gold. The alchemist only responded that he must "go and try." The

Englishman feels annoyed to get such vague instructions after his long journey, but he resolves to try.

Fatima arrives after the Englishman leaves, and Santiago tells her he loves her. As the war drags on and the caravan remains in Al-Fayoum, Santiago meets Fatima at the well every day. Santiago tells Fatima about his Personal Legend which is leading him to the pyramids, but he says he wants to stay in Al-Fayoum with her. One day, Fatima tells Santiago that she has been waiting for him her entire life, but insists that he continue on to Egypt after the war to pursue his Personal Legend. She says if they are meant to be together, they will meet again.

After this conversation, Santiago seeks out the Englishman and discovers he has built a furnace. The Englishman explains that he has abandoned his fear of failure and will attempt the Master Work.

ANALYSIS

In this section, we finally meet the alchemist. He watches the caravan arrive from afar, instead of greeting it along with the tribal chiefs. He acts more like an observer than an involved member of the power structure of Al-Fayoum. In fact, as the old man that Santiago speaks to explains, the chieftains can't even meet with the alchemist unless he consents. Like Melchizedek, the alchemist appears to possess magical powers. He knows in advance that an apprentice will arrive and has supposedly lived for much longer than a typical human lifespan. When Santiago and the Englishman begin asking local residents about the alchemist, the locals react strangely, telling the pair to leave or give up. Some aren't even sure that such a man exists, or at least they try to make the pair believe that he doesn't exist. It remains unclear why the alchemist possesses such a reputation, but he appears to be a powerful and mysterious figure.

Santiago has no purpose for remaining at the oasis, but he ends up benefiting from his time there. Although he knows the alchemist lives there, he doesn't have as much interest in the alchemist as does the Englishman. At first, he even considers the delay in Al-Fayoum a major impediment to his quest for his Personal Legend and evidence that his "beginner's luck" has run out. But Santiago comes to realize that each challenge he faces on the way to his destination forms part of God's plan. Rather than worrying about a schedule he cannot control, he contents himself with remaining at the oasis and opens himself to new experiences. Santiago then meets Fatima. As soon as Santiago approaches her, he notices her beauty, and he falls instantly in love with her. Once the two begin speaking, the delay at the oasis allows them to become friends, and Santiago even starts to worry that one day he will have to leave. He comes to recognize the time as a part of his journey rather than an obstacle, suggesting that fate predestined the delay.

The love affair between Santiago and Fatima moves very quickly, but this suddenness makes sense given the novel's allegorical style. Santiago goes from meeting Fatima to proposing to her in just a few pages. The novel skips any realistic description of the relationship that would develop, nor does it explain their love to the reader. Instead, the book regards Santiago and Fatima's relationship as a symbolic step in Santiago's larger quest for his Personal Legend. He explains their love, for instance, by comparing it to the pure "Language of the World," which allows people (and things) to communicate with each other and with the Soul of the World. The novel treats their love as part of this mysterious process, evident when Santiago recognizes without even speaking to Fatima that he loves her. Consequently, Santiago and Fatima's relationship serves to reiterate the novel's broader themes of interconnectedness and Santiago's growing connection with the forces that bind the world together.

Section 8

Summary

Santiago watches a pair of hawks attacking each other and has a vision of armies riding through the oasis. Santiago remembers Melchizedek's advice to heed omens, so he tells the camel driver about his vision. The camel driver takes Santiago's warning seriously because he believes that all people can penetrate to the Soul of the World.

The camel driver considers how seers make their living by understanding the Soul of the World and recalls a time when a seer asked him why he wanted to know the future. The camel driver had trouble coming up with a good answer, so the seer refused to cast the twigs he used to make his predictions. Instead, he told the camel driver to forget about the future and pay attention to the present. The seer told him that God will occasionally reveal the future to someone, but only so it can be rewritten.

Because the camel driver believes that God showed Santiago the future through his vision, he tells Santiago to warn the local tribal chieftains of approaching armies. Santiago doubts the chieftains will take him seriously, but the camel driver explains that they deal often with omens.

The chieftains reside in a huge white tent in the middle of the oasis. Santiago visits and tells a guard that he saw an omen. The guard goes inside the tent and emerges with a young Arab dressed in white and gold. Santiago explains his vision to the Arab, and the Arab asks Santiago to wait as he goes back into the tent. Santiago waits outside until nightfall, when finally the guard invites him inside. The chieftains sit at the back of the lushly decorated tent on silk pillows, eating, smoking from hookahs, and drinking tea. One of the chieftains asks Santiago why the desert would speak to him, a newcomer to the desert. Santiago replies that, because he is new, he can see things those accustomed to the desert may not. The chieftains argue in an Arabic dialect Santiago can't understand.

The old man at the center of the chieftains, dressed in white and gold, does not speak until the conversation ends. Then he recounts the story of a man who believed in dreams and was sold as a slave. The tribe's merchants bought the man and delivered him to Egypt, because they thought that anyone who believed in dreams could also interpret them. The man was Joseph, and he saved Egypt from famine by interpreting the Pharaoh's dreams. The old man says that the tribe believes in this tradition, which means they must take messages from the desert seriously.

After his speech, the old man says he will lift the ban on carrying weapons in the oasis for one day, and that everyone should be on the lookout for enemies. He says he will reward each man in the oasis for every ten enemies he kills, and if Santiago turns out to be wrong, they will kill him.

Analysis

The vision Santiago has while watching the hawks shows his progress in penetrating to the Soul of the World. In the moments just before Santiago has his vision, he wonders about Fatima and watches a pair of hawks in the sky. He deliberately tries to read meaning into the hawks' flight, and he thinks to himself that he understands the Language of the World better, in part because of his love for Fatima. He feels that everything begins to make sense just as his vision occurs, suggesting that Santiago is, in fact, learning to understand the Language of the World. In addition, the omens Santiago previously experienced offered only vague hints about the course he should take. For instance, his dream about the treasure in Egypt pointed him in the direction of the pyramids but did not give him any detail about what the treasure contained or where it was buried. This new vision, however, gives Santiago a clear and specific image of the future, and unlike Santiago's other visions, which informed his own Personal Legend, the vision of the hawks has implications for the entire oasis. He sees an army riding into the oasis with swords drawn, indicating that an attack will occur soon and allowing the people of the oasis to prepare.

Santiago's decision to go to the tribal chieftains with his knowledge of the future also shows his growing confidence in his ability to understand the Language of the World. Although Santiago has acted on omens regularly, he always hesitates to do so. Here, again, he hesitates. After he has his vision, he wishes he could forget it and return to thinking about Fatima. But he never questions the validity of what he saw. With a little encouragement from the camel driver, Santiago goes to see the chieftains, worrying that they will laugh at him but not that he will turn out to be wrong. He even gives the chieftains a reason why the desert might grant the vision to him rather than one of the men who has always lived in the desert, suggesting he believes in the truth of his vision. Even after the chieftains warn Santiago that they will kill him if he turns out to be wrong, he feels he made the right decision in going to see them.

The camel driver's story about his own experiences going to a seer emphasizes the conflicting points of view we see regarding fate in the novel. According to the camel driver, a seer told him that God only reveals the future if God wrote that future to be altered. If the seer is correct, then the future can, in fact, be changed. Melchizedek suggests as much in his earlier statement to Santiago that the greatest lie ever written is that fate controls people's lives. This notion, however, clashes with the idea that God has already written everything, a belief put forth by various characters and evident in the repetition of the word *maktub*, meaning "it is written." While some characters suggest that God has already determined the course that everything will take, others suggest that each person controls his or her own destiny. The seer appears to fall somewhere in between. He implies that most of the time the future is fixed, but God can choose to reveal it on occasion in order to change it.

SECTION 9

SUMMARY

Santiago leaves the chieftains. Outside, a horseman in black carrying a sword knocks Santiago to the ground. The horseman asks who dared read the flight of the hawks. Santiago says he did and that he was able to see into the Soul of the World. The horseman asks Santiago why he defies Allah's will, and Santiago replies that Allah willed his vision to occur. The horseman withdraws his sword and asks why Santiago is in the desert. When Santiago says he is following his Personal Legend, the horseman explains he needed to test Santiago's courage, and that Santiago must not give up on his goal. The horseman tells Santiago to find him the next day after sunset if he survives the ensuing battle. Santiago asks the horseman where he lives, and the horseman simply points south before riding away. We learn that the mysterious horseman is the alchemist.

The next morning, two thousand armed men guard Al-Fayoum. Five hundred mounted troops arrive in the city pretending to be on a peaceful expedition, but when they arrive at the tent in the center of Al-Fayoum they all draw hidden swords and attack. The tent, however, is empty, and because the tribe is ready, the tribesmen defeat the attackers, killing everyone but the battalion's commander. The chieftains question the commander about why he broke with tradition and attacked Al-Fayoum, and the commander replies that his men were starving and needed to take the oasis to continue with the war. The chieftains express pity but condemn the commander to death by hanging. The old man who leads the chieftains rewards Santiago with fifty gold pieces and asks him to become the tribal counselor.

That night, Santiago wanders to the south of Al-Fayoum. He sees a tent that a group of passing Arabs says genies inhabit. Santiago waits beside the tent, and at midnight the alchemist appears on his horse carrying two dead hawks on his shoulder. The alchemist says Santiago should not be there unless his Personal Legend directed him to. He signals for Santiago to enter the tent. Inside, Santiago sees no traditional alchemy tools. The alchemist tells Santiago that he asked him to come to his tent because the omens told him Santiago would need help. Santiago tells the alchemist that the Englishman needs his help, but the alchemist replies that the Englishman has other things to do first. The alchemist says he needs to help direct Santiago to the treasure he seeks.

Santiago argues that he already has his treasure with his camel, money, and Fatima. The alchemist replies that Santiago has nothing from the pyramids. He proceeds to pour Santiago some wine, even though the rules of Al-Fayoum prohibit drinking alcohol. He tells Santiago to sell his camel and buy a horse.

ANALYSIS

Santiago—and the reader—finally meet the alchemist in this section. The alchemist never actually calls himself "the alchemist," but his identity becomes clear nonetheless. He appears to Santiago in dramatic fashion, dressed all in black, riding a white horse, and kicking up a cloud of dust so large it obscures the moon. This entrance reminds Santiago of Santiago Matamoros, otherwise known as Saint James the Greater, the apostle and patron saint of Spain. Initially, Santiago thinks the man on the horse may kill him, but he feels no fear because he would die in pursuit of his Personal Legend. Since he does not worry about death, Santiago confidently tells the man that he stands behind his vision. The man appears impressed. When he withdraws his sword, he talks about the Language of the World, and Santiago realizes the horseman is not a random enemy come to kill him. Santiago says the man reminds of him of Melchizedek, and as the man rides away the narrator informs us that Santiago has just met the alchemist.

The fact that Santiago's vision of the approaching army comes true the next day confirms that he has penetrated to the Soul of the World. As a result, the tribal chieftains gain a great deal of confidence in Santiago and his abilities, and they ask him to serve as a tribal counselor. Perhaps more importantly, Santiago gains more confidence in his abilities. When the alchemist questions Santiago with his sword drawn, this confidence allows Santiago to speak about his vision with courage. Santiago's response impresses the alchemist, who says he needed to test Santiago's bravery. He also says that courage is the quality most essential to understanding the Language of the World. With this additional confidence in himself, Santiago seems only likely to improve his abilities.

The alchemist's choice to make Santiago his protégé marks an important point in Santiago's journey, and the fact that the alchemist chooses Santiago, despite the fact that Santiago is not interested in alchemy, reiterates the notion that all things are one to people in touch with the Soul of the World. When we first meet the alchemist, we learn that he awaits someone whom he will teach. Meanwhile, the Englishman, who studies alchemy, seeks the alchemist. Despite this apparent match, and the fact that Santiago does not study alchemy, we learn that the alchemist waits for Santiago, not the Englishman. In the world of the book, all pursuits resemble one another in that they involve perfecting a Personal Legend and discovering the Soul of the World. Thus, even though the Englishman seems like the more appropriate pupil, the alchemist chooses Santiago because he is the more advanced student of the Language of the World. When the alchemist says the universe conspires to help people realize their dreams, Santiago recognizes the alchemist as another omen, directing him toward his Personal Legend. Santiago argues that he already has his treasure, including his money and Fatima, but the alchemist points out that none of these things come from the pyramids. Again, Santiago hesitates briefly to pursue his dream because he feels satisfied with the wealth he has. The alchemist, however, pushes him forward.

SECTION 10

SUMMARY

Santiago returns to the alchemist's tent the next night with a horse. The alchemist mounts his own horse and puts a falcon on his shoulder. He tells Santiago to lead him to where there is life in the desert. Santiago feels confused, but he understands what to do when the alchemist tells him that life attracts life. He gallops into the desert until his horse slows down. He tells the alchemist life exists where they have stopped, because his horse knows life. The pair look around among the desert stones, and the alchemist finds a cobra and grabs it by the tail. The cobra flails and hisses, and Santiago jumps away. The alchemist draws a circle in the sand with his scimitar and places the cobra inside it. The cobra relaxes, and the alchemist says the cobra will not leave the circle.

The alchemist prepares to move on with Santiago to the pyramids, but Santiago complains that he doesn't want to leave Fatima. The alchemist says Fatima understands that Santiago needs to complete his Personal Legend. Santiago asks the alchemist what would happen if he stayed in Al-Fayoum. The alchemist explains that Santiago would have enough money to buy many sheep and camels, and that he would marry Fatima. Santiago and Fatima would be happy for one year, but that during the second year Santiago would start to think about the treasure again. He would not be able to ignore the omens. During the third year, Santiago would become increasingly obsessed with his Personal Legend, and Fatima would feel bad for having interrupted Santiago's quest. Santiago and Fatima would still love each other, but by the fourth year, the omens of treasure would disappear. The tribal chieftains would dismiss Santiago as their counselor, and Santiago would live the rest of his life in regret. The alchemist's story convinces Santiago. The pair return to Al-Fayoum for one night, and Santiago tells Fatima he is leaving but that he still loves her and will return. The two embrace, touching for the first time.

The alchemist leads the boy through the desert with the falcon on his shoulder. During their stops, the falcon flies off and returns with rabbits or birds to eat. They travel for a week, speaking little. On the seventh day, the alchemist sets up camp early and tells Santiago his journey is almost finished. Santiago feels frustrated that the alchemist hasn't taught him anything, but the alchemist says Santiago should have learned through actions. Santiago asks him why he is an alchemist, and the alchemist explains he learned the practice from his grandfather when alchemy was simpler. He says men complicated alchemy by writing books about it. Previously, alchemists only needed the Emerald Tablet. Santiago asks what the tablet says, and the alchemist replies that one can't understand it through reason since it provides a passage to the Soul of the World. The alchemist encourages Santiago to immerse himself in the desert and listen to his heart so he can also gain an understanding of the Soul of the World.

ANALYSIS

Santiago's first challenge, to find life in the desert, demonstrates his increasing proficiency at getting in touch with the Soul of the World and also reaffirms elements of the novel's belief system. The alchemist gives Santiago only a vague hint about how to find life in the desert (he says that life attracts life), but immediately Santiago understands the alchemist's meaning. Santiago quickly finds the cobra, and the alchemist considers Santiago's success as a sign of Santiago's ability to understand the Language of the World. Notably, as Santiago gets better at performing these feats, he does not pray or communicate directly with spirits. Instead, he interacts with natural things such as the desert and his horse, emphasizing that the Soul of the World is not an abstract or independent spirit. It exists in every natural thing, and one just needs to develop the right frame of mind to find it.

In this section, we again see Santiago hesitating to pursue his Personal Legend because he feels satisfied with what he already has. Santiago wonders whether he should leave Al-Fayoum at all, and as a result, the alchemist draws the book's sharpest distinction yet between feeling content in the present and feeling a sense of lifelong contentment. According to the alchemist, if Santiago does not pursue his Personal Legend, his relationship with Fatima will eventually deteriorate as she begins to feel he gave up his dream for her and he begins to regret his decision. Moreover, Santiago will gradually lose touch with the Soul of the World. He will lose his ability to recognize omens, and he will no longer serve as tribal counselor to the chieftains of the oasis. The story of Santiago's potential future shows that, though Santiago undoubtedly loves Fatima, that love will not sustain him permanently, suggesting that love holds less spiritual importance than one's Personal Legend. Only by following his Personal Legend will Santiago find lasting satisfaction and avoid regret.

We additionally learn some detail about the alchemist's personal history, about alchemy in general, and about how a person should follow his Personal Legend. Notably, we learn that the alchemist came to alchemy by happenstance. As he tells Santiago, his grandfather was an alchemist and taught him to be one, just as his grandfather learned because his own father was an alchemist, and so on. In other words, the practice of alchemy holds no special significance in the book except as a metaphor for a person's purification in pursuit of his or her Personal Legend. Only the Emerald Tablet serves as an exception to this idea because, as the alchemist tells Santiago, the wisdom it contains provides a direct passage to the Soul of the World. Over time, however, other men trying to become alchemists have complicated that wisdom. They have also sought only the treasure of their Personal Legends, meaning the gold they wanted to create, without actually living out their Personal Legends, and thus lost the ability to practice alchemy. The alchemist's story tells Santiago that the process of pursuing his Personal Legend is more important than the particular dream he wants to fulfill, and that he cannot reach his goal through learning. Santiago must do so through action.

SECTION 11

SUMMARY

Santiago and the alchemist travel cautiously over the next two days while they pass through the area where the tribal fighting is worst. Santiago tells the alchemist his heart doesn't want him to continue because it fears it will lose everything. The alchemist replies that no heart suffers while it pursues its dreams, because to pursue a dream is to encounter God. The next morning, Santiago's heart tells him that everyone who has God within him feels happy, and that everyone on earth has a treasure waiting for him. Santiago tells the alchemist he has made peace with his heart.

The next day, three tribesmen approach Santiago and the alchemist. They insist on searching the pair and discover that the alchemist carries the Philosopher's Stone and the Elixir of Life. The tribesmen laugh when the alchemist tells them about the magical properties of his possessions, and they allow the two to continue on their way. Santiago asks the alchemist why he told the men about his possessions, and the alchemist replies that people seldom believe a person carrying treasures.

As the pair travel, Santiago's heart says it protected him throughout his life in ways he never noticed. They pass a tribal encampment, and Santiago says he feels no danger. The alchemist gets angry, saying that Santiago should remember he travels through the desert. Two men suddenly appear behind Santiago and the alchemist and tell them they can travel no farther. The alchemist stares into the eyes of the men and tells them he and the boy are not going far, and the men leave. The alchemist explains to Santiago that the eyes demonstrate the strength of one's soul.

After the alchemist and Santiago cross a mountain range, the alchemist says that they have two days' remaining on their journey to the pyramids. Santiago asks the alchemist to tell him the secret of alchemy before the two part ways, and the alchemist says Santiago already knows alchemy because he can penetrate to the Soul of the World. Santiago asks how to specifically turn lead into gold. The alchemist says that gold represents the most evolved metal, and that successful alchemists understand evolution.

That evening, hundreds of Arab tribesmen dressed in blue approach Santiago and the alchemist and accuse them of acting as spies. They take them to a military camp and begin questioning them. The alchemist says Santiago is an alchemist and offers

Santiago's money to the tribe's chief. After the chief accepts the money, the alchemist says that Santiago has the power to destroy the camp with the force of the wind. The men laugh and challenge Santiago to prove the alchemist's claim. The alchemist says that after three days Santiago will transform himself into the wind. Santiago feels confused, and the alchemist says he was only trying to avoid getting killed. Santiago replies that, since he can't become the wind, they will die in three days. The alchemist pours tea on Santiago's wrists, saying only fear prevents someone from living out their Personal Legend.

ANALYSIS

As Santiago continues his journey with the alchemist, he learns several new lessons about himself and his abilities. First, the alchemist explains that each person's heart emerges from the Soul of the World. Because Santiago's heart connects him to the Soul of the World, Santiago must learn to listen to it properly. Santiago's heart does not always influence him in positive ways, though. It expresses fear, yearns for Fatima, and otherwise distracts Santiago from following his Personal Legend. Santiago goes as far as to call his heart a traitor, and wonders why he should listen to such a discouraging thing. The alchemist explains that the heart never stays silent, so Santiago must come to terms with it. In other words, Santiago must learn to separate himself from the desires of his heart. Only by paying attention to his heart and understanding its "dodges and tricks" can Santiago tame it and turn it into an ally.

The alchemist teaches Santiago two additional lessons during the pair's ensuing encounters with tribesmen. He admits to the first set of tribesmen that he carries two legendary treasures, the Philosopher's Stone and the Elixir of Life, in order to show Santiago that most people do not believe someone who possesses great treasures. Though the alchemist refers to his material treasures, this lesson can also apply to intangible treasures, such as spiritual knowledge of dreams and omens. In another lesson, the alchemist snaps at Santiago for forgetting that they are in a dangerous place. Santiago, who has tamed his heart and feels no fear, prompts this reaction by the alchemist when he says he does not feel worried about the camp of tribesmen they pass. The alchemist reminds Santiago that the Soul of the World doesn't regard him as any more special than anyone else, causing Santiago to think to himself that everything is one. As if to prove this point to Santiago, two men ride up on Santiago and the alchemist and only leave when the alchemist persuades them to go.

The third encounter Santiago and the alchemist have with tribesmen does not end as easily as the first two, mainly because the alchemist seems to cause trouble deliberately. He gives away all of Santiago's money, for instance, then claims that Santiago has the power to destroy their camp and turn himself into the wind to prove it. The alchemist appears to do this to test Santiago, and while Santiago has faced tests previously on his journey to his Personal Legend, including surviving in Tangier and finding life in the desert with the alchemist, this test will be by far the greatest he has faced. Santiago has only three days to face down his fear of failing and learn to turn himself into the wind. At this point in the story, Santiago doesn't have any idea how to do this. But as the alchemist has told him, no instruction manual can guide him. He must learn by doing.

Section 12

Summary

A battle takes place during Santiago and the alchemist's first day at the camp. Santiago finds the alchemist feeding his falcon and tells him he has no idea how to turn into the wind. He asks why the alchemist doesn't seem worried, since if Santiago doesn't turn into the wind, they will both die. The alchemist says Santiago already knows how to turn himself into the wind.

For most of the second day, Santiago sits on a cliff contemplating his fear. On the third day the chief and his officers visit Santiago to see if he can make good on his claim. Santiago looks out to the desert and it speaks to him. Santiago tells the desert about his love for Fatima, and it offers its sand to Santiago to help the wind blow. It says that Santiago will also have to ask the wind for help.

A breeze picks up as Santiago asks the wind for help. The wind argues that Santiago differs too much from it, but Santiago contends that he desires to reach all corners of the world, just like the wind. The wind understands but doesn't know what to do. Santiago tells the wind that love can empower it to do anything. The wind feels like Santiago demeans what it already knows how to do. It blows harder, annoyed, and tells Santiago to talk to the Hand That Wrote All. Santiago says he will, but that first the wind should create a sandstorm so he can look into the sky without the sun blinding him.

The wind picks up into a powerful gale called the *simum* and the tribesmen ask their chief if they can stop Santiago's stunt. The chief, however, wants to see Santiago complete his task. Santiago speaks to the sun. The sun tells him it knows of love, but Santiago argues it does not. Santiago says that all things have their own Personal Legend, and when something realizes its Personal Legend, it must change so it can acquire a new Personal Legend. Alchemists use this process to coax lead into becoming gold. After hearing Santiago's words, the sun decides to shine more brightly, and the wind blows harder so it can continue to block out the brightness.

Santiago tells the sun that love transforms the Soul of the World and asks the sun to turn him into the wind. The sun says it can't and suggests Santiago speak to the Hand That Wrote All. The wind is happy to see the limit to the sun's wisdom and blows harder. Santiago communicates with the Hand That Wrote All but senses he should not speak. Instead, he prays and experiences a rush of love. He realizes that the Soul of God is his own soul and that he can perform miracles.

Generations of people thereafter remember the wind on that day. When the tribesmen look at where Santiago was standing, he is gone. Instead, he stands far on the other side of camp. The men feel terrified, and the alchemist seems pleased. The chief lets Santiago and the alchemist continue on their journey and provides them with an escort party.

ANALYSIS

Santiago's great test of turning himself into the wind serves as the climactic scene of *The Alchemist*. In this scene, several of the novel's major themes and symbols converge. Santiago, for instance, must overcome his fear, a theme the novel presents as a person's greatest obstacle in pursuit of his Personal Legend. He also communicates with the desert, one of the most prominent symbols in the novel. Repeatedly in *The Alchemist,* the desert acts both as a challenge to Santiago and a teacher. It poses threats, such as the wars, but the desert also teaches Santiago to understand the Language of the World as he spends more and more time contemplating it. He uses this knowledge to communicate with different elements within this scene, including the desert itself, the wind, and the sun. In the context of the novel, Santiago can communicate with all these elements because they all speak the Language of the World and because they are all part of the Soul of the World, again emphasizing the theme of unity across all elements in nature. Additionally, Santiago recognizes that each element has its own Personal Legend, even inanimate objects. Invoking the main symbol of the book, he explains that alchemy involves coaxing lead to live out its Personal Legend of evolving into gold. Finally, Santiago, in something like his notion of alchemy, transforms himself literally into the wind.

This physical transformation adds a new dimension to the ideas of alchemy and the Personal Legend that we have seen up to this point in the novel. Previously, alchemy had generally referred to a spiritual transformation brought about when one reached his or her Personal Legend. Here, however, achieving one's Personal Legend causes a physical transformation with implications beyond the individual. Santiago tells the sun that once something achieves its Personal Legend, it evolves into something new and better and assumes a new Personal Legend. As the elements of the world evolve in this way, they grow like a pyramid into "one thing only," the highest step of evolution. If every natural thing completes the cycle of achieving its Personal Legend, evolving and repeating the cycle, eventually all creation will become the same thing. According to Santiago, this evolutionary spirituality allows for alchemy and for personal transformation. It also roots Santiago's seemingly selfish quest to find a treasure in the higher goal of becoming part of a unified creation.

Santiago's challenge also reiterates the alchemist's lesson that knowledge must be gained through action. As Santiago prepares to attempt to turn himself into the wind, the alchemist offers him little, if any, help. The alchemist goes so far as to say he will be safe in any case since he can already become the wind, but that he won't protect Santiago if he fails. The alchemist's behavior suggests that Santiago must face this test alone, without assistance or even instruction from the alchemist. In fact, repeatedly in the novel we see teachers, such as the alchemist and Melchizedek, and omens, such as Santiago's initial dream of the treasure, providing only limited guidance to Santiago. Most of what he accomplishes in the story he does primarily on his own.

SECTION 13

SUMMARY: SECTION 13

Santiago, the alchemist, and their escort ride until they arrive at a Coptic monastery. The alchemist tells Santiago they are three hours from the pyramids, and that he must finish the trip alone. The alchemist speaks to one of the monks in a strange language, and the monk leads them to the kitchen and brings them a block of lead. The alchemist heats it and shaves off a sliver of the Philosopher's Stone. He adds the lead sliver to the pan, and the mixture becomes red. When it dries, it is gold. Santiago wants to try but the alchemist reminds him that alchemy is not his Personal Legend. The alchemist gives gold to the monk, to Santiago, and keeps some himself. He also gives a fourth part to the monk to keep for Santiago.

Before leaving, the alchemist tells Santiago a story about Emperor Tiberius of Rome. Tiberius had one son who was a soldier and one who was a poet. An angel tells him in a dream that generations of men will know the words of one of his sons. After Tiberius dies, he meets the angel from his dream and thanks the angel for saying his son's poetry would become immortal. The angel replies that people have forgotten his son's poetry. Instead, the son who was a soldier met the Son of God while looking for a healer for his servant. The soldier said that he was not worthy and that the Son of God needed only to speak one word and his servant would be healed. These words became immortal.

Santiago rides off alone. As a full moon rises, Santiago sees the pyramids from atop a dune. He falls to his knees and sees a scarab in the sand. He starts digging in that spot but finds nothing. Eventually, two refugees from the tribal wars approach and yank Santiago from the hole. They take his gold, and assuming Santiago is digging toward more gold, force him to keep digging until morning. When Santiago finds nothing, they beat him until he nearly dies. Santiago gasps that he saw the treasure in a dream, which makes the attackers think he is crazy. One tells Santiago he had a dream of a treasure buried in Spain, and describes the church and sycamore tree from Santiago's days as a shepherd. The attacker says he isn't stupid enough to pursue it. Santiago smiles. He knows where to find his treasure.

SUMMARY: EPILOGUE

Santiago arrives at the church and falls asleep contemplating the strange way God has guided him to the treasure. He wakes up digging and laughing about how God left gold at the monastery through the alchemist to ease his journey back. A voice in the wind says God wanted him to see the pyramids' beauty. Soon Santiago finds a chest of gold coins and jewels. He removes Urim and Thummim and puts them in the chest. He plans to head to Tarifa and give the Gypsy one tenth of his treasure, and as the wind blows he feels Fatima's kiss on his lips. Santiago declares that he will return to her soon.

ANALYSIS

The story that the alchemist tells Santiago about Emperor Tiberius and his sons appears to hold the lesson that, although a person may not have a destiny he expects or even desires, if that person acts in accordance with his own desires, he will serve a purpose greater than himself. In the story, which appears in the Bible in Matthew 8:5-8, a centurion demonstrates his faith in Jesus, acknowledging that if Jesus just speaks a word he can heal the centurion's servant, who is paralyzed and suffering. The angel tells Tiberius that, although the centurion did not intend to be remembered for this speech, his words have become immortal. This story reiterates the notion that in living out his Personal Legend, Santiago served not only himself but also the Soul of the World. Also, just like the Narcissus story from the beginning of *The Alchemist,* this story takes a well-known narrative, this time a story from the Bible, and adds another dimension to it, giving it a new meaning in the context of the novel.

Some of the events from earlier in the book foreshadow Santiago's final challenge at the pyramids and his ultimate return to Spain. Santiago, for instance, learns about the importance of omens involving scarabs earlier in his trip, and the scarab he sees near the pyramids shows him where to dig. Of course, Santiago doesn't find anything where he sees the scarab, but the location happens to be in the path of the men who will assault him later and reveal to him the true location of the treasure. In addition, when Santiago's attackers scoff at him for pursuing a treasure from a dream, the episode parallels the earlier incident in which the alchemist admits to the tribesman that he was carrying the Philosopher's Stone and Elixir of Life. Like the alchemist, Santiago expresses an earnest belief in the knowledge he carries, and that belief essentially saves him by making his attackers think he is crazy.

The final twist, that the treasure lies under the sycamore tree in Spain the whole time, brings Santiago back home, just as his father predicted when Santiago first set out on his travels as a shepherd. Most notably, however, this detail also reiterates the alchemist's lesson about the alchemists who have lost the ability to turn lead to gold. These men, the alchemist says, want just the treasure from their Personal Legends without actually living out their Personal Legends. For Santiago, the value of his journey does not lie in the treasure at the end, but in the knowledge and experience he gains from the journey itself. The fact that the treasure contains actual gold and jewels seems almost incidental, though it does emphasize the point made earlier in the novel that pursuing one's Personal Legend can also lead to material wealth.

IMPORTANT QUOTATIONS EXPLAINED

1. "...whoever you are, or whatever it is that you do,
    when you really want something, it's because that desire
    originated in the soul of the universe. It's your mission
    on earth."

This statement, which Melchizedek says to Santiago upon their first meeting, forms the foundation of the philosophy of The Alchemist. Essentially, Melchizedek says that dreams are not silly or selfish desires that should be ignored. Instead, they serve as the primary means by which people can get in touch with the mystical force that connects everything in the universe. He convinces Santiago that his nagging desire to visit the pyramids is actually a calling, and he sets Santiago on his journey of spiritual discovery. By associating seemingly selfish human desires with the soul of the universe, *The Alchemist* presents a form of spirituality that differs radically from traditional religions that espouse self-denial. Instead of practicing sympathy by identifying with and helping others, Santiago must focus on his own personal dreams.

This quote also introduces the concept of the soul of the universe, which characters refer to later in the novel as the Soul of the World. This entity becomes extremely important later in the book, as it is the spirit that Santiago must connect with in order to turn into the wind. The quote alludes to the idea that a person's purpose in life centers on fulfilling one's desires, a notion that also becomes important in the form of the Personal Legend. Although this quotation doesn't mention these ideas by name, it lays the groundwork for Santiago's and the reader's later understanding of them.

2. "...every blessing ignored becomes a curse. I don't want
    anything else in life. But you are forcing me to look at
    wealth and at horizons that I have never known. Now
    that I have seen them, and now that I see how immense my
    possibilities are, I'm going to feel worse than I did before

you arrived. Because I know the things I should be able to accomplish, and I don't want to do so."

The crystal merchant says these words to Santiago as Santiago prepares to leave Tangier after an extremely successful year working at the crystal shop. The crystal merchant expresses a regret common to several ancillary characters in *The Alchemist,* such as the baker and Santiago's father. He knows that he has not achieved all he can in life and feels depressed as a result. The crystal merchant serves as a warning to Santiago that those who ignore their Personal Legends in favor of settling into material comforts always feel haunted by their untapped potential. This idea recurs throughout the book, and the complacency that the crystal merchant represents serves as a constant danger for Santiago. Santiago nearly goes back to Spain after leaving Tangier, for instance, and he hesitates to leave the Al-Fayoum oasis for the pyramids because he already has Fatima and some wealth there.

The characters that guide Santiago, most notably the alchemist, constantly warn him against settling for what he has. The alchemist, for instance, describes how Santiago's life would unfold if he remained at the oasis rather than live out his Personal Legend. Santiago and Fatima would be happy for some time, but gradually Santiago would begin to regret not seeking out his Personal Legend, while Fatima would feel that she caused Santiago to abandon his dreams. Eventually, Santiago would no longer be able to read omens, and he would ultimately lose touch with the Soul of the World. The lesson set forth in the quotation and in this subsequent example essentially is that a person can only feel truly fulfilled by pursuing his or her Personal Legend.

3.   "We are afraid of losing what we have, whether it's our life or our possessions or our property. But this fear evaporates when we understand that our life stories and the history of the world were written by the same hand."

Here, the camel driver addresses fear while he tells Santiago his life story during the trip to Al-Fayoum. Fear acts as the biggest impediment to achieving one's Personal Legend. Santiago faces many obstacles during his journey, but he regularly feels tempted to abandon his quest when he fears losing what he has already earned. For example, Santiago initially balks at giving up his flock of sheep to Melchizedek. In Tangier, Santiago fears losing the money he earned with the crystal merchant. In the oasis, Santiago fears losing Fatima. Finally, after being captured, Santiago fears he will never be able to turn into the wind. The irony of these fears stems from the fact that Santiago earns ever greater rewards each time he abandons his fear and gives up his previous possessions.

This quotation also raises the notion that a person should have no reason to fear anything if he recognizes that he plays a role in something greater than his own life. The camel driver speaks these lines to Santiago from experience, having lost all of his possessions when a flood destroyed his orchard farm. He acknowledges, however, that the same hand that writes a person's life story also writes the history of the world. In other words, each person's life plays a part in the larger world around him, and the camel driver suggests that God dictates that part. This realization doesn't prevent a person from suffering tragedies, but if the person recognizes that his tragedy serves a higher purpose, he has no reason to fear any loss. This insight becomes important to Santiago as he faces challenges later in the book, particularly as he learns to stop fearing failure and to trust in the omens he sees.

4. "The alchemists spent years in their laboratories, observing the fire that purified the metals. They spent so much time close to the fire that gradually they gave up the vanities of the world. They discovered that the purification of the metals had led to a purification of themselves."

The Englishman relates this history to Santiago as Santiago reads a book on alchemy. The quotation summarizes the key insight that connects the practice of transforming metals through alchemy with the idea of human beings attaining spiritual perfection by pursuing their Personal Legends. Just as alchemists purify lead, removing its impurities to transform it into gold, a person can purify himself by focusing completely on living out his Personal Legend. This process strips the person of impurities, transforming him as the lead is transformed. Similarly, the alchemists the Englishman speaks of did not purify themselves because they wanted to create gold but because they became so focused on their Personal Legends that they rid themselves of all other concerns, "the vanities of the world" as the Englishman puts it.

Santiago's guides through *The Alchemist*, including Melchizedek and the alchemist himself, stress to Santiago that he must also put aside all other concerns. The alchemist counsels Santiago to leave the oasis, for instance, even though Santiago wants to stay for Fatima. But abandoning these other cares acts as the equivalent of removing impurities from lead, and only by remaining committed foremost to living out his Personal Legend will Santiago transform himself. This idea implies that all other desires, including that for romantic love, should play a secondary role to pursuing one's Personal Legend.

5.   'What you still need to know is this: before a dream is realized, the Soul of the World tests everything that was learned along the way. It does this not because it is evil, but so that we can, in addition to realizing our dreams, master the lessons we've learned as we've moved toward that dream. That's the point at which, as we say in the language of the desert, one 'dies of thirst just when the palm trees have appeared on the horizon.'
    "Every search begins with beginner's luck. And every search ends with the victor being severely tested."

The alchemist says these last words to Santiago before the two part ways at the end of the novel. In short, the alchemist explains to Santiago why he had to endure so many trials if the universe, as the alchemist and others have said, does actually want him to fulfill his Personal Legend. Santiago, for instance, may have begun his journey with "beginner's luck," although only to a limited degree, as he was immediately robbed and left penniless in Tangier, but as his quest went on he faced progressively more difficult challenges. When he must turn himself into the wind, it seems as if Santiago has to trick the elements into helping him. But as the alchemist explains, these challenges serve their own purpose: to help Santiago master the lessons he has already learned.

The alchemist's statement implies that the important part of pursuing one's Personal Legend consists not just in reaching the final goal, whether that be turning lead into gold or finding a treasure near the pyramids, but also in learning through action. Earlier in the book, the alchemist explained this notion to Santiago using alchemists themselves as his example. He said the alchemists became too focused on the gold and lost the focus on living out their Personal Legends. As a result, they lost the ability to perform alchemy. Santiago, meanwhile, ultimately travels through Spain, into Africa, and across the Sahara to the pyramids, only to learn that the treasure he seeks lies under a tree in the area where he began his trip. His transformation, however, could not have occurred without his journey and the experience he gained from living out his Personal Legend. Along the way, he learned to read omens, to communicate with the elements, and even to turn himself into the wind.

KEY FACTS

FULL TITLE
The Alchemist

AUTHOR
Paulo Coelho

TYPE OF WORK
Novel

GENRE
Fiction

LANGUAGE
Portuguese

TIME AND PLACE WRITTEN
1988, Brazil

DATE OF FIRST PUBLICATION
1988

PUBLISHER
The original publisher was a small Brazilian publishing house; Rocco, another Brazilian publishing company, was the first large publisher to print the book. HarperOne is the American Publisher.

NARRATOR
The narrator is an anonymous omniscient observer. The narrator speaks in a simple tone and knows the thoughts and feelings of every character in the book.

POINT OF VIEW
The point of view is third person omniscient, though the narrator focuses on Santiago's journey. Occasionally, the narration will step back from Santiago and focus on an ancillary character, but it always returns to its protagonist. Notably, the narrator stops referring to Santiago after the first third of the book. Though the point of view comments on some of the characters' innermost thoughts and desires, it is a mostly objective observer.

TONE

> *The Alchemist* reads like an ancient myth or fable. It is simple, direct, and overtly didactic. It also has elements of a picaresque, an episodic tale detailing a hero's adventures during his quest.

TENSE

> The story is told in the past tense.

SETTING (TIME)

> *The Alchemist* is set in an indistinct time in the past. It is clearly a pre-modern time, before cars and most modern technology existed.

SETTING (PLACE)

> The main plot of *The Alchemist* takes place in the Spanish pastures, the Spanish town of Tarifa, the city of Tangier in North Africa, and the Sahara Desert.

PROTAGONIST

> The novel's protagonist is Santiago, an Andalusian shepherd.

MAJOR CONFLICT

> The major conflict of the book is Santiago's personal tension between completing his Personal Legend to travel all the way to Egypt to find a treasure at the pyramids and settling along the way for the treasures he has already earned.

RISING ACTION

> Santiago makes a series of material sacrifices in order to pursue his Personal Legend to reach the pyramids of Egypt.

CLIMAX

> Santiago struggles to turn himself into the wind while being held by warring tribesmen in the Sahara Desert.

FALLING ACTION

> Santiago arrives at the pyramids, but in a twist, he must go back to Spain, after he learns that his treasure was buried in an abandoned church by a sycamore tree where he started his journey.

THEMES

> The Centrality of Personal Legends; The Unity of Nature; The Danger of Fear

KEY FACTS

MOTIFS

Dreams; *Maktub*; Omens

SYMBOLS

Santiago's Sheep; Alchemy; The Desert

FORESHADOWING

One piece of foreshadowing occurs when Santiago has his
initial dream of the pyramids under the sycamore tree. Later,
we learn that the treasure he saw in his dream is buried under
that very tree. As story progresses, Melchizedek foreshadows
Santiago's success with the crystal merchant when he explains
the notion of "beginner's luck." Additionally, the innocuous
run-ins Santiago and the alchemist have with various tribesmen
in the desert foreshadow Santiago and the alchemist's
eventual capture. Finally, Santiago's ongoing envy of the wind
foreshadows his climactic effort to turn himself into it.

STUDY QUESTIONS & ESSAY TOPICS

STUDY QUESTIONS

1. *How does the story of Narcissus relate to the broader message of* THE ALCHEMIST?

The myth of Narcissus usually ends when Narcissus becomes so thoroughly entranced by his own reflection that he falls into the lake and drowns. In the novel's version of the myth, however, we learn that the lake felt upset because Narcissus died, since it enjoyed looking at its own reflection in Narcissus's eyes. This version of the myth presents a more complicated picture of vanity than the original. As opposed to being an undesirable trait that leads to death, vanity appears to be an entirely natural characteristic, so much so that the lake displays it.

Like the introductory Narcissus story, *The Alchemist* itself has a message that focusing on oneself can connect a person to nature and the spiritual world. Only through singlemindedly pursuing his own Personal Legend does Santiago learn the secrets of the Soul of the World, for instance. Repeatedly throughout the book, Santiago must put his own interests first as when he chooses to be a shepherd rather than a priest and when he leaves the oasis to continue his journey. But by disregarding everything but his own dream, Santiago realizes his true potential. In this way, he penetrates to the Soul of the World.

2. *What attitude does* THE ALCHEMIST *take toward romantic love?*

Unlike many popular literary tales, *The Alchemist* initially presents love not as a goal, but as an obstacle. Santiago says his initial love of the merchant's daughter acts as the only thing that makes him want to stay in one place forever. This desire stands in direct opposition to the journey he must complete in order to fulfill his Personal Legend.

When Santiago finds his true love, Fatima, at the oasis, he feels even more convinced to abandon his Personal Legend. Fatima and the alchemist must show Santiago that his dream holds more importance than staying with her.

This picture of love is unique compared to traditional illustrations of romantic love. For one, this love is completely distinct from possession. Santiago has a significant internal dialogue about this distinction, and he puts it to the test when he leaves Fatima. Love, in *The Alchemist,* is also secondary to pursuing one's Personal Legend. As the alchemist tells Santiago, Santiago's love for Fatima will only survive if he continues living out his Personal Legend so that he will have no regrets later. Despite these facts, which seem to downplay the importance of love, Fatima's kiss serves as the final image of the book, suggesting that love remains necessary for Santiago to live a contented life.

3.   *What is the attitude of* THE ALCHEMIST *toward material wealth and individualism, and how does it differ from major world religions in this regard?*

Unlike many religions, *The Alchemist* does not draw a distinction between the material and the spiritual worlds. The book also espouses individuality as a means of achieving the ultimate goals of creation. Additionally, elements of pantheism appear throughout the book. For one, Santiago communicates with and finds omens in natural entities such as the desert and the wind. The alchemist says that these elements have Personal Legends just as humans do, and that they were also born from the Soul of the World. The alchemist also associates the process of purifying metal into gold with spiritual purification.

The book's dominant strain of evolutionary spirituality appears most clearly when Santiago tries to turn himself into the wind. In the context of the novel, when an element or individual pursues a Personal Legend, it will evolve into a higher state of being. The goal of creation consists of all nature, humans and inanimate objects included, undergoing this evolution until the universe achieves perfection. This philosophy differs from traditional spirituality in that it requires everything pursuing its individual dream to achieve this state rather than practicing selflessness. In fact, the novel even portrays religious characters who practice self-denial, such as the crystal merchant, as failures.

Suggested Essay Topics

1. *How does Santiago's spiritual journey parallel the alchemist's practice of transforming metal into gold?*

2. *What are the weaknesses that Santiago sees in his flock of sheep, and how do they relate to the weaknesses of human beings who fail to pursue their Personal Legends?*

3. *According to the book, is it possible to live a fulfilling life without ever achieving one's Personal Legend? Why or why not?*

4. *What role do forces of nature such as the wind and the sun play in Santiago's journey?*

5. *During Santiago's stay in Tangier, what does Santiago teach the crystal merchant, and what does the crystal merchant teach Santiago?*

6. *What stylistic strategies does Coelho use to make* The Alchemist *come across as a mythic, universally applicable story?*

7. *What is the function of magic in* The Alchemist, *and what does the ability to practice magic symbolize?*

QUESTIONS & ESSAYS

How to Write
Literary Analysis

The Literary Essay: A Step-by-Step Guide

When you read for pleasure, your only goal is enjoyment. You might find yourself reading to get caught up in an exciting story, to learn about an interesting time or place, or just to pass time. Maybe you're looking for inspiration, guidance, or a reflection of your own life. There are as many different, valid ways of reading a book as there are books in the world.

When you read a work of literature in an English class, however, you're being asked to read in a special way: you're being asked to perform *literary analysis*. To analyze something means to break it down into smaller parts and then examine how those parts work, both individually and together. Literary analysis involves examining all the parts of a novel, play, short story, or poem—elements such as character, setting, tone, and imagery—and thinking about how the author uses those elements to create certain effects.

A literary essay isn't a book review: you're not being asked whether or not you liked a book or whether you'd recommend it to another reader. A literary essay also isn't like the kind of book report you wrote when you were younger, where your teacher wanted you to summarize the book's action. A high school- or college-level literary essay asks, "How does this piece of literature actually work?" "How does it do what it does?" and, "Why might the author have made the choices he or she did?"

The Seven Steps

No one is born knowing how to analyze literature; it's a skill you learn and a process you can master. As you gain more practice with this kind of thinking and writing, you'll be able to craft a method that works best for you. But until then, here are seven basic steps to writing a well-constructed literary essay:

> 1. *Ask questions*
> 2. *Collect evidence*
> 3. *Construct a thesis*

4. *Develop and organize arguments*
5. *Write the introduction*
6. *Write the body paragraphs*
7. *Write the conclusion*

1. Ask Questions

When you're assigned a literary essay in class, your teacher will often provide you with a list of writing prompts. Lucky you! Now all you have to do is choose one. Do yourself a favor and pick a topic that interests you. You'll have a much better (not to mention easier) time if you start off with something you enjoy thinking about. If you are asked to come up with a topic by yourself, though, you might start to feel a little panicked. Maybe you have too many ideas—or none at all. Don't worry. Take a deep breath and start by asking yourself these questions:

- **What struck you?** Did a particular image, line, or scene linger in your mind for a long time? If it fascinated you, chances are you can draw on it to write a fascinating essay.

- **What confused you?** Maybe you were surprised to see a character act in a certain way, or maybe you didn't understand why the book ended the way it did. Confusing moments in a work of literature are like a loose thread in a sweater: if you pull on it, you can unravel the entire thing. Ask yourself why the author chose to write about that character or scene the way he or she did and you might tap into some important insights about the work as a whole.

- **Did you notice any patterns?** Is there a phrase that the main character uses constantly or an image that repeats throughout the book? If you can figure out how that pattern weaves through the work and what the significance of that pattern is, you've almost got your entire essay mapped out.

- **Did you notice any contradictions or ironies?** Great works of literature are complex; great literary essays recognize and explain those complexities. Maybe the title (*Happy Days*) totally disagrees with the book's subject matter (hungry orphans dying in the woods). Maybe the main character acts one way around his family and a completely different way around his friends and associates. If you can find a way to explain a work's contradictory elements, you've got the seeds of a great essay.

At this point, you don't need to know exactly what you're going to say about your topic; you just need a place to begin your exploration. You can help direct your reading and brainstorming by formulating your topic as a *question,* which you'll then try to answer in your essay. The best questions invite critical debates and discussions, not just a rehashing of the summary. Remember, you're looking for something you can *prove or argue* based on evidence you find in the text. Finally, remember to keep the scope of your question in mind: is this a topic you can adequately address within the word or page limit you've been given? Conversely, is this a topic big enough to fill the required length?

GOOD QUESTIONS
"Are Romeo and Juliet's parents responsible for the deaths of their children?"
"Why do pigs keep showing up in LORD OF THE FLIES?*"*
"Are Dr. Frankenstein and his monster alike? How?"

BAD QUESTIONS
"What happens to Scout in TO KILL A MOCKINGBIRD?*"*
"What do the other characters in JULIUS CAESAR *think about Caesar?"*
"How does Hester Prynne in THE SCARLET LETTER *remind me of my sister?"*

---

2. COLLECT EVIDENCE
Once you know what question you want to answer, it's time to scour the book for things that will help you answer the question. Don't worry if you don't know what you want to say yet—right now you're just collecting ideas and material and letting it all percolate. Keep track of passages, symbols, images, or scenes that deal with your topic. Eventually, you'll start making connections between these examples and your thesis will emerge.

Here's a brief summary of the various parts that compose each and every work of literature. These are the elements that you will analyze in your essay, and which you will offer as evidence to support your arguments. For more on the parts of literary works, see the Glossary of Literary Terms at the end of this section.

ELEMENTS OF STORY   These are the *what*s of the work—what happens, where it happens, and to whom it happens.

- **Plot:** All of the events and actions of the work.
- **Character:** The people who act and are acted upon in a literary work. The main character of a work is known as the *protagonist*.
- **Conflict:** The central tension in the work. In most cases, the protagonist wants something, while opposing forces (antagonists) hinder the protagonist's progress.
- **Setting:** When and where the work takes place. Elements of setting include location, time period, time of day, weather, social atmosphere, and economic conditions.
- **Narrator:** The person telling the story. The narrator may straightforwardly report what happens, convey the subjective opinions and perceptions of one or more characters, or provide commentary and opinion in his or her own voice.
- **Themes:** The main idea or message of the work—usually an abstract idea about people, society, or life in general. A work may have many themes, which may be in tension with one another.

ELEMENTS OF STYLE   These are the *how*s—how the characters speak, how the story is constructed, and how language is used throughout the work.

- **Structure and organization:** How the parts of the work are assembled. Some novels are narrated in a linear, chronological fashion, while others skip around in time. Some plays follow a traditional three- or five-act structure, while others are a series of loosely connected scenes. Some authors deliberately leave gaps in their works, leaving readers to puzzle out the missing information. A work's structure and organization can tell you a lot about the kind of message it wants to convey.
- **Point of view:** The perspective from which a story is told. In *first-person point of view*, the narrator involves him or herself in the story. ("I went to the store"; "We watched in horror as the bird slammed into the window.") A first-person narrator is usually the protagonist of the work, but not always. In *third-person point of view*, the narrator does not participate

in the story. A third-person narrator may closely follow a specific character, recounting that individual character's thoughts or experiences, or it may be what we call an *omniscient* narrator. Omniscient narrators see and know all: they can witness any event in any time or place and are privy to the inner thoughts and feelings of all characters. Remember that the narrator and the author are not the same thing!

- **Diction:** Word choice. Whether a character uses dry, clinical language or flowery prose with lots of exclamation points can tell you a lot about his or her attitude and personality.

- **Syntax:** Word order and sentence construction. Syntax is a crucial part of establishing an author's narrative voice. Ernest Hemingway, for example, is known for writing in very short, straightforward sentences, while James Joyce characteristically wrote in long, incredibly complicated lines.

- **Tone:** The mood or feeling of the text. Diction and syntax often contribute to the tone of a work. A novel written in short, clipped sentences that use small, simple words might feel brusque, cold, or matter-of-fact.

- **Imagery:** Language that appeals to the senses, representing things that can be seen, smelled, heard, tasted, or touched.

- **Figurative language:** Language that is not meant to be interpreted literally. The most common types of figurative language are *metaphors* and *similes,* which compare two unlike things in order to suggest a similarity between them— for example, "All the world's a stage," or "The moon is like a ball of green cheese." (Metaphors say one thing *is* another thing; similes claim that one thing is *like* another thing.)

3. Construct a Thesis

When you've examined all the evidence you've collected and know how you want to answer the question, it's time to write your thesis statement. A *thesis* is a claim about a work of literature that needs to be supported by evidence and arguments. The thesis statement is the heart of the literary essay, and the bulk of your paper will be spent trying to prove this claim. A good thesis will be:

- **Arguable.** "*The Great Gatsby* describes New York society in the 1920s" isn't a thesis—it's a fact.

- **Provable through textual evidence.** "*Hamlet* is a confusing but ultimately very well-written play" is a weak thesis because it offers the writer's personal opinion about the book. Yes, it's arguable, but it's not a claim that can be proved or supported with examples taken from the play itself.

- **Surprising.** "Both George and Lenny change a great deal in *Of Mice and Men*" is a weak thesis because it's obvious. A really strong thesis will argue for a reading of the text that is not immediately apparent.

- **Specific.** "Dr. Frankenstein's monster tells us a lot about the human condition" is *almost* a really great thesis statement, but it's still too vague. What does the writer mean by "a lot"? *How* does the monster tell us so much about the human condition?

GOOD THESIS STATEMENTS

Question: In *Romeo and Juliet*, which is more powerful in shaping the lovers' story: fate or foolishness?

Thesis: "Though Shakespeare defines Romeo and Juliet as 'star-crossed lovers' and images of stars and planets appear throughout the play, a closer examination of that celestial imagery reveals that the stars are merely witnesses to the characters' foolish activities and not the causes themselves."

Question: How does the bell jar function as a symbol in Sylvia Plath's *The Bell Jar*?

Thesis: "A bell jar is a bell-shaped glass that has three basic uses: to hold a specimen for observation, to contain gases, and to maintain a vacuum. The bell jar appears in each of these capacities in *The Bell Jar*, Plath's semi-autobiographical novel, and each appearance marks a different stage in Esther's mental breakdown."

Question: Would Piggy in *The Lord of the Flies* make a good island leader if he were given the chance?

Thesis: "Though the intelligent, rational, and innovative Piggy has the mental characteristics of a good leader, he ultimately lacks the social skills necessary to be an effective one. Golding emphasizes this point by giving Piggy a foil in the charismatic Jack, whose magnetic personality allows him to capture and wield power effectively, if not always wisely."

LITERARY ANALYSIS

4. Develop and Organize Arguments

The reasons and examples that support your thesis will form the middle paragraphs of your essay. Since you can't really write your thesis statement until you know how you'll structure your argument, you'll probably end up working on steps 3 and 4 at the same time.

There's no single method of argumentation that will work in every context. One essay prompt might ask you to compare and contrast two characters, while another asks you to trace an image through a given work of literature. These questions require different kinds of answers and therefore different kinds of arguments. Below, we'll discuss three common kinds of essay prompts and some strategies for constructing a solid, well-argued case.

Types of Literary Essays

- **Compare and contrast**

  Compare and contrast the characters of Huck and Jim in The Adventures of Huckleberry Finn.

  Chances are you've written this kind of essay before. In an academic literary context, you'll organize your arguments the same way you would in any other class. You can either go *subject by subject* or *point by point*. In the former, you'll discuss one character first and then the second. In the latter, you'll choose several traits (attitude toward life, social status, images and metaphors associated with the character) and devote a paragraph to each. You may want to use a mix of these two approaches—for example, you may want to spend a paragraph apiece broadly sketching Huck's and Jim's personalities before transitioning into a paragraph or two that describes a few key points of comparison. This can be a highly effective strategy if you want to make a counterintuitive argument—that, despite seeming to be totally different, the two objects being compared are actually similar in a very important way (or vice versa). Remember that your essay should reveal something fresh or unexpected about the text, so think beyond the obvious parallels and differences.

- **Trace**

  Choose an image—for example, birds, knives, or eyes—and trace that image throughout Macbeth.

  Sounds pretty easy, right? All you need to do is read the play, underline every appearance of a knife in *Macbeth,* and then list them in your essay in the order they appear, right? Well, not exactly. Your teacher doesn't want a simple catalog of examples. He or she wants to see you make *connections* between those examples—that's the difference between summarizing and analyzing. In the *Macbeth* example above, think about the different contexts in which knives appear in the play and to what effect. In *Macbeth,* there are real knives and imagined knives; knives that kill and knives that simply threaten. Categorize and classify your examples to give them some order. Finally, always keep the overall effect in mind. After you choose and analyze your examples, you should come to some greater understanding about the work, as well as your chosen image, symbol, or phrase's role in developing the major themes and stylistic strategies of that work.

- **Debate**

  Is the society depicted in 1984 good for its citizens?

  In this kind of essay, you're being asked to debate a moral, ethical, or aesthetic issue regarding the work. You might be asked to judge a character or group of characters (*Is Caesar responsible for his own demise?*) or the work itself (*Is* JANE EYRE *a feminist novel?*). For this kind of essay, there are two important points to keep in mind. First, don't simply base your arguments on your personal feelings and reactions. Every literary essay expects you to read and analyze the work, so search for evidence in the text. What do characters in *1984* have to say about the government of Oceania? What images does Orwell use that might give you a hint about his attitude toward the government? As in any debate, you also need to make sure that you define all the necessary terms before you begin to argue your case. What does it mean to be a "good" society? What makes a novel "feminist"? You should define your terms right up front, in the first paragraph after your introduction.

  Second, remember that strong literary essays make contrary and surprising arguments. Try to think outside the box. In the *1984* example above, it seems like the obvious answer would be no, the totalitarian society depicted in Orwell's novel is *not* good for its citizens. But can you think of any arguments for the opposite side? Even if your final assertion is that the novel depicts a cruel, repressive, and therefore harmful society, acknowledging and responding to the counterargument will strengthen your overall case.

LITERARY ANALYSIS

5. WRITE THE INTRODUCTION

Your introduction sets up the entire essay. It's where you present your topic and articulate the particular issues and questions you'll be addressing. It's also where you, as the writer, introduce yourself to your readers. A persuasive literary essay immediately establishes its writer as a knowledgeable, authoritative figure.

An introduction can vary in length depending on the overall length of the essay, but in a traditional five-paragraph essay it should be no longer than one paragraph. However long it is, your introduction needs to:

- **Provide any necessary context.** Your introduction should situate the reader and let him or her know what to expect. What book are you discussing? Which characters? What topic will you be addressing?

- **Answer the "So what?" question.** Why is this topic important, and why is your particular position on the topic noteworthy? Ideally, your introduction should pique the reader's interest by suggesting how your argument is surprising or otherwise counterintuitive. Literary essays make unexpected connections and reveal less-than-obvious truths.

- **Present your thesis.** This usually happens at or very near the end of your introduction.

- **Indicate the shape of the essay to come.** Your reader should finish reading your introduction with a good sense of the scope of your essay as well as the path you'll take toward proving your thesis. You don't need to spell out every step, but you do need to suggest the organizational pattern you'll be using.

Your introduction should not:

- **Be vague.** Beware of the two killer words in literary analysis: *interesting* and *important*. Of course the work, question, or example is interesting and important—that's why you're writing about it!

- **Open with any grandiose assertions.** Many student readers think that beginning their essays with a flamboyant statement such as, "Since the dawn of time, writers have been fascinated with the topic of free will," makes them sound important and commanding. You know what? It actually sounds pretty amateurish.

- **Wildly praise the work.** Another typical mistake student writers make is extolling the work or author. Your teacher doesn't need to be told that "Shakespeare is perhaps the greatest writer in the English language." You can mention a work's reputation in passing—by referring to *The Adventures of Huckleberry Finn* as "Mark Twain's enduring classic," for example—but don't make a point of bringing it up unless that reputation is key to your argument.

- **Go off-topic.** Keep your introduction streamlined and to the point. Don't feel the need to throw in all kinds of bells and whistles in order to impress your reader—just get to the point as quickly as you can, without skimping on any of the required steps.

---

6. WRITE THE BODY PARAGRAPHS

Once you've written your introduction, you'll take the arguments you developed in step 4 and turn them into your body paragraphs. The organization of this middle section of your essay will largely be determined by the argumentative strategy you use, but no matter how you arrange your thoughts, your body paragraphs need to do the following:

- **Begin with a strong topic sentence.** Topic sentences are like signs on a highway: they tell the reader where they are and where they're going. A good topic sentence not only alerts readers to what issue will be discussed in the following paragraph but also gives them a sense of what argument will be made *about* that issue. "Rumor and gossip play an important role in *The Crucible*" isn't a strong topic sentence because it doesn't tell us very much. "The community's constant gossiping creates an environment that allows false accusations to flourish" is a much stronger topic sentence— it not only tells us *what* the paragraph will discuss (gossip) but *how* the paragraph will discuss the topic (by showing how gossip creates a set of conditions that leads to the play's climactic action).

- **Fully and completely develop a single thought.** Don't skip around in your paragraph or try to stuff in too much material. Body paragraphs are like bricks: each individual

one needs to be strong and sturdy or the entire structure
will collapse. Make sure you have really proven your point
before moving on to the next one.

- **Use transitions effectively.** Good literary essay writers know
  that each paragraph must be clearly and strongly linked to
  the material around it. Think of each paragraph as a response
  to the one that precedes it. Use transition words and phrases
  such as *however, similarly, on the contrary, therefore,* and
  furthermore to indicate what kind of response you're making.

---

7. WRITE THE CONCLUSION

Just as you used the introduction to ground your readers in the topic
before providing your thesis, you'll use the conclusion to quickly
summarize the specifics learned thus far and then hint at the broader
implications of your topic. A good conclusion will:

- **Do more than simply restate the thesis.** If your thesis argued
  that *The Catcher in the Rye* can be read as a Christian
  allegory, don't simply end your essay by saying, "And that
  is why *The Catcher in the Rye* can be read as a Christian
  allegory." If you've constructed your arguments well, this
  kind of statement will just be redundant.

- **Synthesize the arguments, not summarize them.** Similarly,
  don't repeat the details of your body paragraphs in your
  conclusion. The reader has already read your essay, and
  chances are it's not so long that they've forgotten all your
  points by now.

- **Revisit the "So what?" question.** In your introduction,
  you made a case for why your topic and position are
  important. You should close your essay with the same sort
  of gesture. What do your readers know now that they didn't
  know before? How will that knowledge help them better
  appreciate or understand the work overall?

- **Move from the specific to the general.** Your essay has most
  likely treated a very specific element of the work—a single
  character, a small set of images, or a particular passage. In
  your conclusion, try to show how this narrow discussion has
  wider implications for the work overall. If your essay on *To
  Kill a Mockingbird* focused on the character of Boo Radley,
  for example, you might want to include a bit in your

conclusion about how he fits into the novel's larger message about childhood, innocence, or family life.

- **Stay relevant.** Your conclusion should suggest new directions of thought, but it shouldn't be treated as an opportunity to pad your essay with all the extra, interesting ideas you came up with during your brainstorming sessions but couldn't fit into the essay proper. Don't attempt to stuff in unrelated queries or too many abstract thoughts.

- **Avoid making overblown closing statements.** A conclusion should open up your highly specific, focused discussion, but it should do so without drawing a sweeping lesson about life or human nature. Making such observations may be part of the point of reading, but it's almost always a mistake in essays, where these observations tend to sound overly dramatic or simply silly.

A+ Essay Checklist

Congratulations! If you've followed all the steps we've outlined above, you should have a solid literary essay to show for all your efforts. What if you've got your sights set on an A+? To write the kind of superlative essay that will be rewarded with a perfect grade, keep the following rubric in mind. These are the qualities that teachers expect to see in a truly A+ essay. How does yours stack up?

- ✓ Demonstrates a thorough understanding of the book
- ✓ Presents an original, compelling argument
- ✓ Thoughtfully analyzes the text's formal elements
- ✓ Uses appropriate and insightful examples
- ✓ Structures ideas in a logical and progressive order
- ✓ Demonstrates a mastery of sentence construction, transitions, grammar, spelling, and word choice

A+ Student Essay

In what ways does Santiago receive guidance in the novel?
What do the various guides Santiago encounters suggest
about guidance generally?

Guidance appears to Santiago in various forms. He receives it in
guises as varied as a gypsy woman, a wind, and the desert itself.
As one might expect given these different disguises, guidance isn't
always straightforward or obvious when it does appear. Often the
guidance being offered is abstract, and Santiago is only helped in his
journey when he is able to recognize it as guidance. By employing
these strange and indirect forms of guidance as well as the more
direct ones, however, the novel suggests that guides exist all around
us in order to point us in the right direction. Our ability to benefit
from guidance depends on our willingness to recognize and listen
to it.

Santiago's journey begins with an instruction that he at first
doesn't recognize as guidance, and he has to be educated before
he can learn to recognize the omens that will point him on his way
throughout his life's journey. Each time he sleeps under a certain
sycamore tree, he dreams of a child telling him to find a treasure
at the foot of the pyramids. Initially he doesn't recognize this as
a directive pointing him toward something he should actually do
in his waking life. That realization comes only after he is told, in a
much more direct and conventional form of guidance, by the gypsy
woman and then the mysterious Melchizedek, to travel to Egypt.
He then grasps that his Personal Legend demands he go to the
pyramids and seek out the treasure he envisioned there. During
the course of his journey, the guidance offered by dreams, visions,
and omens becomes apparent to the reader. Notably, when Santiago
later sees the two hawks fighting in the desert, he has a vision of
a war to come. This vision proves to be an important omen for
the tribes living in the area, and the story the tribal chieftains
recount further reinforces the value of listening to dreams. They tell
Santiago that the biblical Joseph, in fact, helped save Egypt because
he believed in dreams and could interpret them. When Santiago
meets the alchemist himself, the alchemist tells him he is helping
Santiago because the omens said he would need it. He also says

Santiago will always be reminded of his Personal Legend if he doesn't pursue it, because the omens will always be there.

Another type of omen that guides Santiago on his quest is the timing of events. At times in his journey, seemingly serendipitous events urge him on, and their timing suggests they are not mere coincidences. It's not until Santiago feels the intense wind, called the levanter, the freedom of which he greatly envies, that he decides to actually buy passage on a boat going to Africa, even though the gypsy woman and Melchizedek had previously told him to. While the wind doesn't necessarily tell Santiago what to do, at least not more than his dreams do, it does remind him of what he wants at a moment when he needs reminding. In that regard it offers him guidance much as the gypsy woman and Melchizedek did. This same sort of serendipitous guidance occurs when Santiago drops the two stones Melchizedek gave him, when he considers returning to life as a shepherd. The stones remind him of his Personal Legend, and because of them he resolves to continue on his journey.

Santiago receives yet another kind of guidance when he is shown what can happen if he gives up pursuing his Personal Legend. Out of fear, the crystal merchant Santiago works for in Tangiers has given up his own dream of traveling to Mecca. As a result, he is deeply unhappy. He serves as a living cautionary tale to Santiago. Moreover, as Santiago travels across the desert with the alchemist, he is given a sense of what his life would be like if married Fatima and stayed in Al-Fayoum without pursuing his Personal Legend. The series of events the alchemist lays out reveals the disappointment and remorse Santiago would ultimately feel. In both cases, he is spurred on by the fear of a life of regret.

Of course, sometimes the guidance takes the very clear form of a character telling Santiago what to do. The gypsy woman, Melchizedek, and the alchemist all have this role.

The guidance Santiago receives all comes down to one lesson, for the most part: Never give up pursuing your Personal Legend. That these diverse types of guidance share the same message for Santiago suggests all of creation, whether it's rocks or the wind or people, is working in concert to push Santiago, and indeed everyone, toward their Personal Legend. In *The Alchemist*, fulfilling one's dreams is a person's greatest responsibility.

GLOSSARY OF LITERARY TERMS

ANTAGONIST
> The entity that acts to frustrate the goals of the *protagonist*. The antagonist is usually another *character* but may also be a non-human force.

ANTIHERO / ANTIHEROINE
> A *protagonist* who is not admirable or who challenges notions of what should be considered admirable.

CHARACTER
> A person, animal, or any other thing with a personality that appears in a *narrative*.

CLIMAX
> The moment of greatest intensity in a text or the major turning point in the *plot*.

CONFLICT
> The central struggle that moves the *plot* forward. The conflict can be the *protagonist*'s struggle against fate, nature, society, or another person.

FIRST-PERSON POINT OF VIEW
> A literary style in which the *narrator* tells the story from his or her own *point of view* and refers to himself or herself as "I." The narrator may be an active participant in the story or just an observer.

HERO / HEROINE
> The principal *character* in a literary work or *narrative*.

IMAGERY
> Language that brings to mind sense-impressions, representing things that can be seen, smelled, heard, tasted, or touched.

MOTIF
> A recurring idea, structure, contrast, or device that develops or informs the major *themes* of a work of literature.

NARRATIVE
> A story.

NARRATOR

The person (sometimes a *character*) who tells a story; the *voice* assumed by the writer. The narrator and the author of the work of literature are not the same person.

PLOT

The arrangement of the events in a story, including the sequence in which they are told, the relative emphasis they are given, and the causal connections between events.

POINT OF VIEW

The *perspective* that a *narrative* takes toward the events it describes.

PROTAGONIST

The main *character* around whom the story revolves.

SETTING

The location of a *narrative* in time and space. Setting creates mood or atmosphere.

SUBPLOT

A secondary *plot* that is of less importance to the overall story but may serve as a point of contrast or comparison to the main plot.

SYMBOL

An object, *character,* figure, or color that is used to represent an abstract idea or concept. Unlike an *emblem,* a symbol may have different meanings in different contexts.

SYNTAX

The way the words in a piece of writing are put together to form lines, phrases, or clauses; the basic structure of a piece of writing.

THEME

A fundamental and universal idea explored in a literary work.

TONE

The author's attitude toward the subject or *characters* of a story or poem or toward the reader.

VOICE

An author's individual way of using language to reflect his or her own personality and attitudes. An author communicates voice through *tone, diction,* and *syntax.*

LITERARY ANALYSIS

A Note on Plagiarism

Plagiarism—presenting someone else's work as your own—rears its ugly head in many forms. Many students know that copying text without citing it is unacceptable. But some don't realize that even if you're not quoting directly, but instead are paraphrasing or summarizing, *it is plagiarism* unless you cite the source.

Here are the most common forms of plagiarism:

- Using an author's phrases, sentences, or paragraphs without citing the source
- Paraphrasing an author's ideas without citing the source
- Passing off another student's work as your own

How do you steer clear of plagiarism? You should *always* acknowledge all words and ideas that aren't your own by using quotation marks around verbatim text or citations like footnotes and endnotes to note another writer's ideas. For more information on how to give credit when credit is due, ask your teacher for guidance or visit www.sparknotes.com.

REVIEW & RESOURCES

QUIZ

1. What does Santiago notice in the sacristy of the abandoned church where he takes shelter on the way to the merchant?

    A.   A burning bush
    B.   Several lost sheep
    C.   A sycamore tree
    D.   A huge wooden cross

2. What did Santiago's parents originally hope he would become when he grew up?

    A.   A lawyer
    B.   A shepherd
    C.   A merchant
    D.   A priest

3. In the recurring dream Santiago has at the abandoned church, who encourages him to seek treasure at the pyramids?

    A.   His mother
    B.   A sheep
    C.   A child
    D.   The merchant's daughter

4. What comforts Santiago when he is visiting the Gypsy dream interpreter?

    A.   An image of Jesus
    B.   A large cross
    C.   A group of teenagers in the waiting room
    D.   Urim and Thummim

5. What does Melchizedek ask Santiago for in return for directing him toward his personal legend?

    A. One tenth of his flock
    B. His cloak
    C. The rest of his gold
    D. The gypsy's phone number

6. Who does Melchizedek point out to Santiago as someone who did not follow his Personal Legend?

    A. A butcher
    B. A baker
    C. A candlestick maker
    D. The dream interpreter

7. What does the book that Santiago buys in Tarifa describe in its opening pages?

    A. A burial ceremony
    B. A desert journey
    C. A fierce battle
    D. A hidden treasure

8. As Santiago sets off to Africa, Melchizedek recalls guiding who else to his Personal Legend?

    A. The alchemist
    B. Jesus
    C. Paulo Coelho
    D. Abraham

9. What distracts Santiago and allows the young man in Tarifa to steal his money?

    A. A beautiful Arab girl
    B. A king adorned with robes
    C. A sword embossed in silver
    D. A stand selling exotic fruits

THE ALCHEMIST 79

10. What kind of vendor does Santiago admire the morning after he is robbed by the young man in Tarifa?

A. A fruit vendor
B. A weaponsmith
C. A bookseller
D. A candy seller

11. What does Santiago suggest to the crystal merchant as a strategy to make more money?

A. Sell tea in crystal glasses
B. Discount crystal on weekends
C. Open a stall in the marketplace
D. Export crystal to Spain

12. According to the Englishman, what is the name of the discovery that is the result of refining metal until all that is left is the Soul of the World?

A. The Universal Legend
B. The Master Work
C. The Voice of the Wind
D. The Hand of God

13. What is the product of alchemy that can turn lead into gold?

A. The Master Work
B. The Alchemist's Furnace
C. The Philosopher's Stone
D. The Elixir of Gold

14. What is the product of alchemy that can cure all illnesses?

A. The Master Work
B. The Philosopher's Stone
C. The Soul of the World
D. The Elixir of Life

REVIEW & RESOURCES

15. Upon what item is the core secret of alchemy written?

   A.   The Holy Grail
   B.   The Emerald Tablet
   C.   The Book of Kings
   D.   The One Ring

16. What surprises Santiago about the Al-Fayoum oasis?

   A.   It is larger than towns in Spain
   B.   Residents dress entirely in black
   C.   All residents speak fluent Spanish
   D.   Strange animals roam the streets

17. Where does Santiago meet Fatima?

   A.   Inside the chieftain's tent
   B.   Next to a well
   C.   Crying in the desert
   D.   In a stable

18. What is the portentous omen that Santiago sees in the Al-Fayoum oasis?

   A.   A pair of hawks fighting
   B.   A dying scarab
   C.   A fast-moving black cloud
   D.   A fierce and sudden windstorm

19. How does the tribal chieftain punish the chief of the invading army?

   A.   Tarring and feathering
   B.   Death by beheading
   C.   Death by hanging
   D.   Banishment from the desert

20. What job does the Al-Fayoum tribal chieftain offer Santiago to reward him for warning of invading armies?

   A.   Army general
   B.   Counselor of the oasis
   C.   Templar commander
   D.   Diplomat to Europe

Suggestions for Further Reading

ARIAS, JUAN. *Paulo Coelho: Confessions of a Pilgrim.* London, HarperCollins: 2001.

COELHO, PAULO. *Warrior of the Light: A Manual,* translated from the Portuguese by Margaret Jull Costa. New York, HarperCollins: 2003.

COELHO, PAULO and KIRKUS REVIEWS. "Q&A: Paulo Coelho." *Kirkus Reviews* 73, no. 11 (1 June 2005): 4.

COELHO, PAULO and SHALAKA PARADKAR, "On The Road." *Gulf News* (April 2007): http://www.gulfnews.com.

COELHO, PAULO and UNESCO COURIER. "The Beyond Is Accessible To Those Who Dare." *Unesco Courier* vol. 51, no. 3 (March 1998): 34-7.

GOODYEAR, DANA. "The Magus: The Astonishing Appeal of Paulo Coelho." *The New Yorker* 83, no. 11 (7 May 2007): 38.

MORAIS, FERNANDO. *Paulo Coelho: A Warrior's Life: The Authorized Biography.* New York, HarperLuxe: 2009.

SEXTON, DAVID. "The High Priest of Spiritual Twaddle." *Evening Standard* (4 August 2003): 35.

WARK, PENNY. "The Meaning of Life? The Joy of Meeting My Many, Many Readers." *Times (London)* (12 April 2007): 8.

REVIEW & RESOURCES